AN ANTHOLOGY OF
OUR EXTRAORDINARY

Earth

Written by Cally Oldershaw

Illustrated by Angela Rizza
and Daniel Long

DK

Introduction

The Earth is constantly changing. Some days are warm and sunny, while others are cold, wet, and stormy. Different weather patterns change the surface of the Earth. Over time, rocks are weathered and eroded, and landscapes change, too. Movements underground can be seen on the surface of Earth – as earthquakes and volcanoes. Over millions of years, mountains form and are worn away.

This minute, a leaf might fall off a tree into a lake, a tiny grain of sand might be blown across a desert, and mineral-rich water might drip into a limestone cave – over millions of years, small differences can cause big changes. As an Earth scientist, I study the way the Earth works, a bit like a detective. You can, too! By finding out how the Earth works now, we can learn about how it worked in the past, and what changes might happen in the future.

Cally Oldershaw

Cally Oldershaw
Author

Contents

Planet Earth

We live on a very special planet, which orbits the Sun along with the other planets of the Solar System. Earth formed about 4.5 billion years ago, and because of our position as the third planet from the Sun, we have water and, therefore, life. Active plate tectonics constantly shape our globe unlike any other planet. We also experience weather, and so this means that our rocky land and sea don't stay the same.

Mountains are worn down by weathering and erosion, and new ones are made where land is pushed together. In other places, the land splits and moves apart, allowing oceans to grow or lava to erupt. Heat from our planet's interior gives us geothermal power, a renewable energy source that can be used to make electricity. Combined with pressure, this same heat forges and transforms rocks. Earth's natural treasures are created, a precious collection including minerals, gemstones, crystals, and metals.

Earth is the only planet in our Solar System that we know has water on its surface, to support life.

Clockwise from top left: Fingal's cave, Scotland; blue and white crystals at the centre of a geode; a Herkimer diamond nestled in bedrock; and textured marble from Italy.

Earth's layers

Atmosphere

As the Earth formed, gases escaped and produced the atmosphere. This is mainly made up of nitrogen, carbon dioxide, and water vapour.

About 4.5 billion years ago, Earth formed. It cooled from a planet of molten magma, and heavier metals sank towards its centre to make the core. Other, lighter, elements didn't sink so far. They formed the mantle and crust layers of the Earth.

Land

The land is the part of the Earth's surface that is not covered by water, but by rocks, soil, and vegetation.

Continents The seven continents of the world are: Asia, Africa, North America, South America, Antarctica, Europe, and Australia.

Ocean

More than 70 per cent of the Earth's surface is covered by fresh or salty water. The water in the world's oceans and seas is salty.

Mantle

The mantle is the layer between the core and the crust. It is mostly made from rock that is rich in iron and magnesium and it is almost 3,000 km (2,000 miles) thick.

Continental crust

The continents are made of continental crust. It is about 40 km (25 miles) thick – much thicker than the oceanic crust.

Inner core

You would need to drill down to about 6,400 km (4,000 miles) to reach the inner core – a solid ball of iron and nickel metals.

Outer core

The liquid outer core wraps around the inner core. It is mostly made from liquid iron, nickel, and oxygen.

Oceanic crust

The oceanic crust is thinner than the continental crust, and is mostly about 7 km (4 miles) thick. Under the oceans, the oldest oceanic crust is around 200 million years old.

Hot rocks The temperature at the centre of the Earth is about 5,200°C (9,392°F).

Core

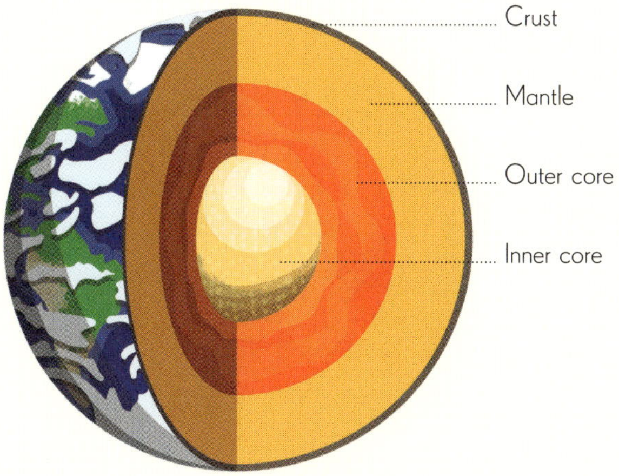

At 5,200°C (9,392°F), the temperature at the centre of Earth is about as hot as the Sun's surface.

If you think of the Earth as an apple, Earth's crust would be as thick as the apple skin. And again like an apple, planet Earth has a core at its centre, only with no stalk! We know that Earth's core is made up of two parts – a sizzling hot, solid inner core, surrounded by a thick layer of liquid. The inner core is about 2,400 km (1,500 miles) wide, and is made of two metals – nickel and iron – while the outer core is made up of mostly liquid iron, nickel, and oxygen.

To get down to the edge of the outer core you would need to dig about 3,000 km (2,000 miles) deep. So far, we have only dug about 12 km (7.5 miles) down into the Earth's crust, so we've still a long way to go.

Earth's inner core is made of the metals nickel and iron, the same as this meteorite that formed at the same time as the Earth.

Kimberlite is a volcanic rock that comes from the mantle. This diamond crystal has been brought to the surface in the kimberlite.

Mantle

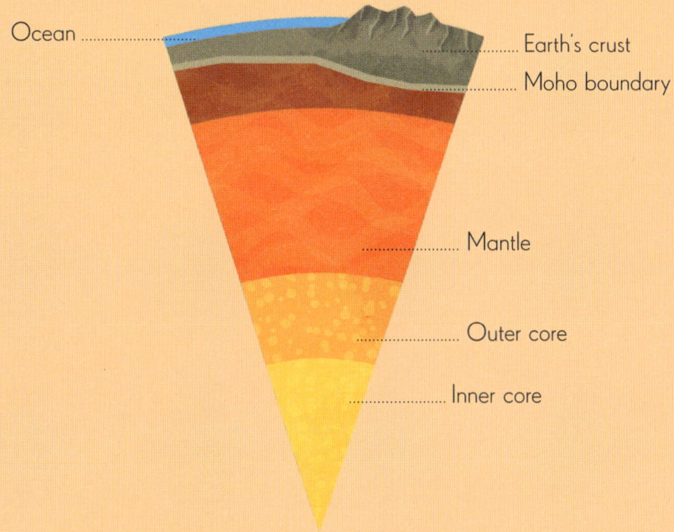

There is a thick layer of rock that comes between Earth's core and its crust. This is called the mantle. It is almost 3,000 km (2,000 miles) thick. Dark mantle rocks have lots of iron and magnesium minerals in them. Some have green olivines and pyroxenes, and even red garnets or diamonds.

The boundary between the mantle and Earth's crust is called the Moho boundary. It is named after the person who studied it – a Croatian scientist called Andrija Mohorovičić. He couldn't actually see the boundary, but he knew it was there. This was because he was studying earthquakes and he noticed they changed speed at a particular depth, which – he realized – must mean they were hitting a different material.

Diamonds form about 160 km (100 miles) below the surface of the Earth.

Granite makes up 80 per cent of Earth's continental crust.

Rocky crust

The magnificent, jagged Torres del Paine mountains soar into the sky in the region of Patagonia in Chile. Their name means "blue towers" and they were made deep underground by movement under the Earth's crust. Twelve million years ago, molten rock called magma had pushed upwards through Earth's layers. However, rather than erupting as a volcano, the magma never reached the surface. Instead, the molten rock cooled underground and formed a rounded dome of granite. During the last Ice Age, about 14,000 years ago, the ground was covered in ice, but as the ice started to melt, the ground and softer sediments on top of the granite were worn away. Then gradually, the granite was worn down until only these distinctive blueish-coloured towers were left.

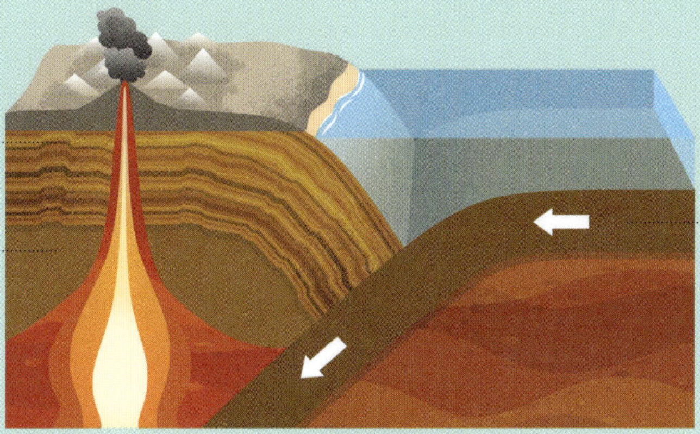

When wet oceanic crust sinks into the mantle, it causes it to melt and form magma. The hot, liquid magma pushes up through the continental crust, where it can erupt as a volcano or cool and form mountains like the Torres del Paine.

The tallest of the three granite towers of Torres del Paine is 2,500 m (8,200 ft). Torres means "towers" in Spanish, and Paine, pronounced PIE-nay, means "blue" in the local Tehuelche (Aonikenk) language of Patagonia.

The Giant's Causeway is made up of about 40,000 columns of volcanic basalt rock.

Giant's path

The Giant's Causeway was created from volcanic lava that rose up at the Mid-Oceanic Ridge.

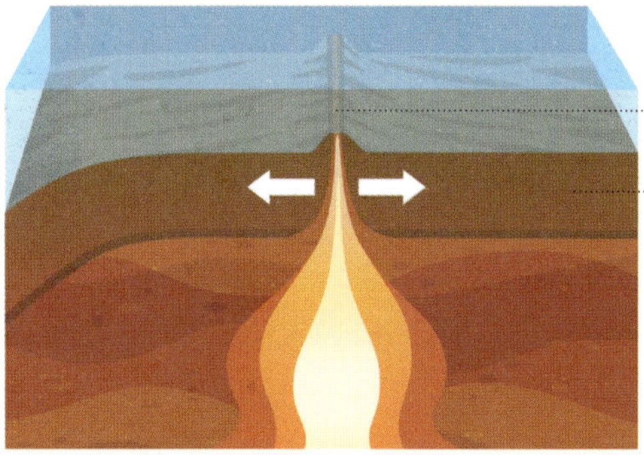

The Giant's Causeway in Northern Ireland has columns reaching up to 12 m (39 ft) in height.

The legend of the Giant's Causeway tells how the Irish giant Finn McCool built a path over the sea from Northern Ireland to Scotland to meet the Scottish giant Benandonner, who had challenged him to a fight. Benandonner lost, and running back to Scotland he destroyed part of the causeway.

The real story behind this extraordinary site is rather different, but just as amazing. The basalt columns that make up the causeway were formed from hot, runny lava that erupted from the oceanic crust about 50–60 million years ago and spread out as a flat plateau. As the lava cooled, it shrank and cracked, forming thousands of mostly hexagonal-shaped columns.

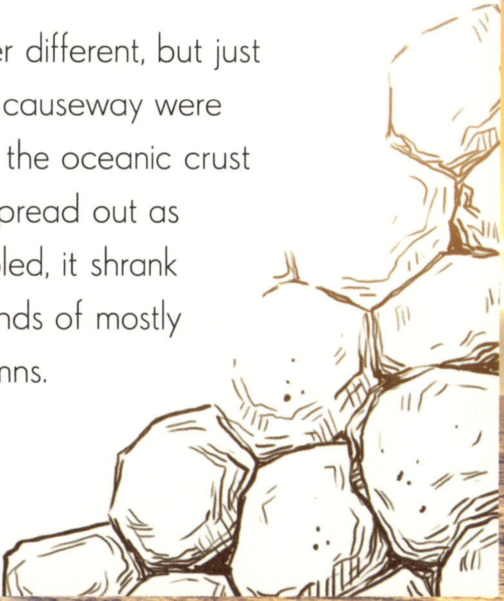

Meteor Crater

The Earth is hit by thousands of meteorites each year, but many land in the sea and are never found.

Fragments of a meteorite created Meteor Crater about 50,000 years ago. The crater is about 1,200 m (3,900 ft) wide and 170 m (560 ft) deep.

Meteors are shooting stars that create bright streaks in the night sky. They are made from rock and space debris that burn up as they travel through Earth's atmosphere. If they land on Earth, they are known as meteorites. If you should happen to see a meteorite land on the ground you have witnessed a "fall". This happens rarely – there have only been about 1,500 falls ever recorded. If a meteorite is found later, this is a "find". There are about 66,000 of these to date, with more waiting to be discovered by meteorite hunters.

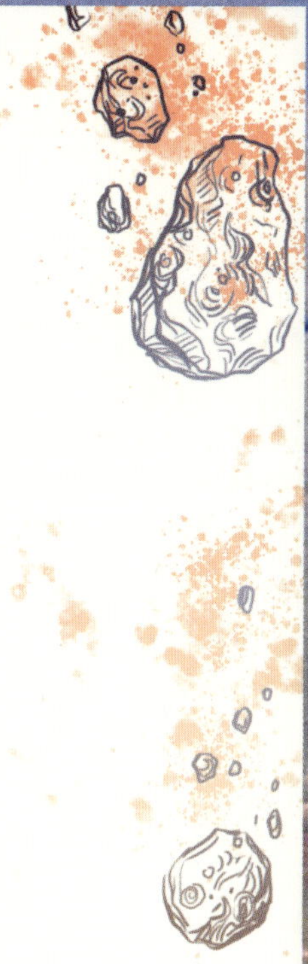

If a meteorite is large enough and travelling fast enough, it can form a crater when it crashes to Earth. One of the biggest is Meteor Crater in Arizona, USA. It is also known as the Barringer Crater, named after the geologist Daniel Barringer, who first discovered that the crater was the result of a meteorite impact.

Weathering

Rocks at the surface are broken down into smaller pieces by water, ice, and wind in a process called weathering.

Cooling

The magma may cool underground or erupt from volcanoes as lava. As the liquid lava or magma cools and hardens, it turns solid and becomes igneous rock.

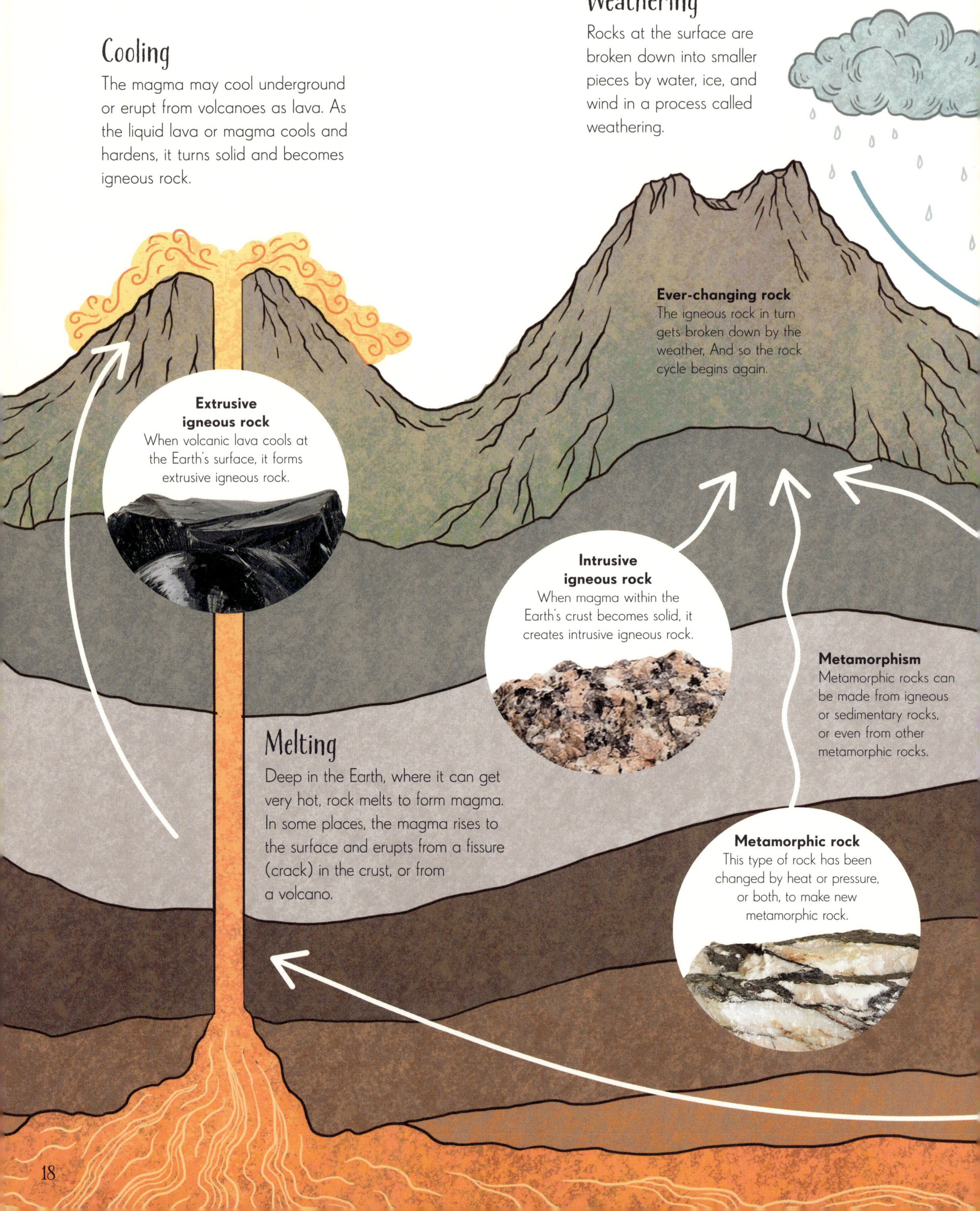

Rock cycle

The Earth is constantly creating and recycling rocks, changing their colours, shapes, and textures. We call this the rock cycle. Geologists sort rocks into three types: igneous, sedimentary, or metamorphic. Each rock type is found at a different stage in the rock cycle.

Erosion

Rocks and rock fragments are further broken down and transported downhill towards the ocean. This process is called erosion.

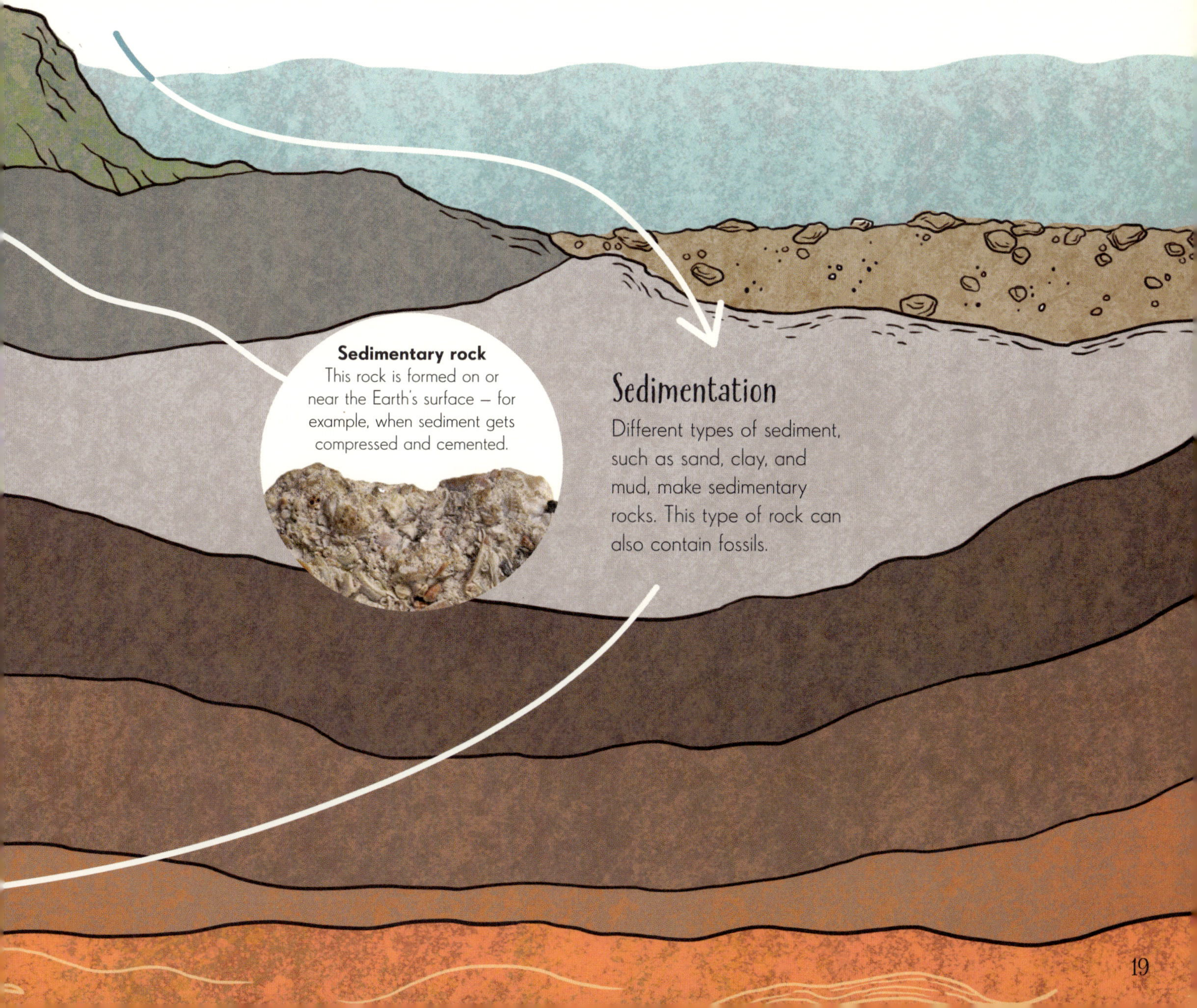

Sedimentary rock
This rock is formed on or near the Earth's surface – for example, when sediment gets compressed and cemented.

Sedimentation

Different types of sediment, such as sand, clay, and mud, make sedimentary rocks. This type of rock can also contain fossils.

Devils Tower is a sacred place to Native American people, who call it the "Bear's Tipi".

Devils Tower

Looming up out of the Black Hills of Wyoming, USA, is an extraordinary sight. Known as Devils Tower, this enormous piece of igneous rock formed about 40 million years ago when volcanic magma cooled and set hard. Originally, the rock lay deep underground, but over millions of years, the softer surrounding layers of sedimentary rock eroded away, leaving the exposed, harder igneous rock. If you look at the picture, you can see hundreds of parallel cracks etched deep into the rock. These cracks divide Devils Tower into huge hexagon columns and help make it one of the most popular climbing destinations in North America.

Devils Tower is made from phonolite. Here are three other types of igneous rock:

Granite

Pumice

Obsidian

Devils Tower in northwest Wyoming is 264 m (867 ft) high, with a flat top about the size of a football pitch.

The Rainbow Mountains are more than 55 million years old.

Rainbow rocks

The glorious Rainbow Mountains in northwest China are aptly named. They are made from layer upon layer of sandstone rock in shades of red, orange, yellow, blue, and purple. Each layer of the sandstone is made up of a mix of sand, mud, and clay, which together are called sediment – and that is why this type of layered rock is called sedimentary.

Sedimentary rocks are formed when sediment is carried by wind, water, and ice, then dropped on dry land or on the beds of rivers, lakes, and seas. Gradually, the layers of sediment build up until they get compacted into rock. This is what happened to the Rainbow Mountains. Over millions of years, the rocks were weathered and the minerals in them changed colour, to give a painter's palette of colours.

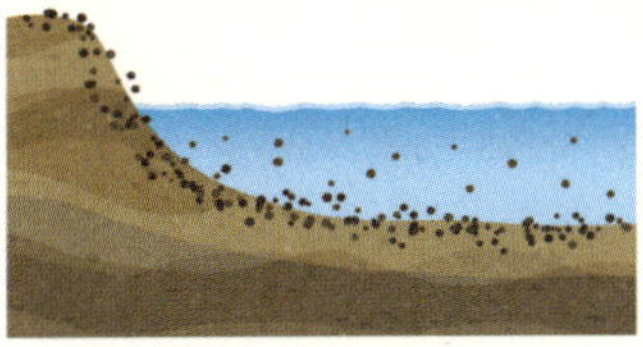

Sedimentary rocks can be formed from sediment settling on riverbeds.

Over time, more sediment settles and layers of rock are formed.

As the layers build, the rock gets pressed down and compacted.

The Rainbow Mountains of the Zhangye Danxia National Geopark in northwest China are coloured by iron and other minerals.

Fossils

After an animal dies, the body gradually rots away.

The skeleton gets buried under layers of earth.

The animal remains get replaced by rock minerals.

Many years later, the fossils are dug up.

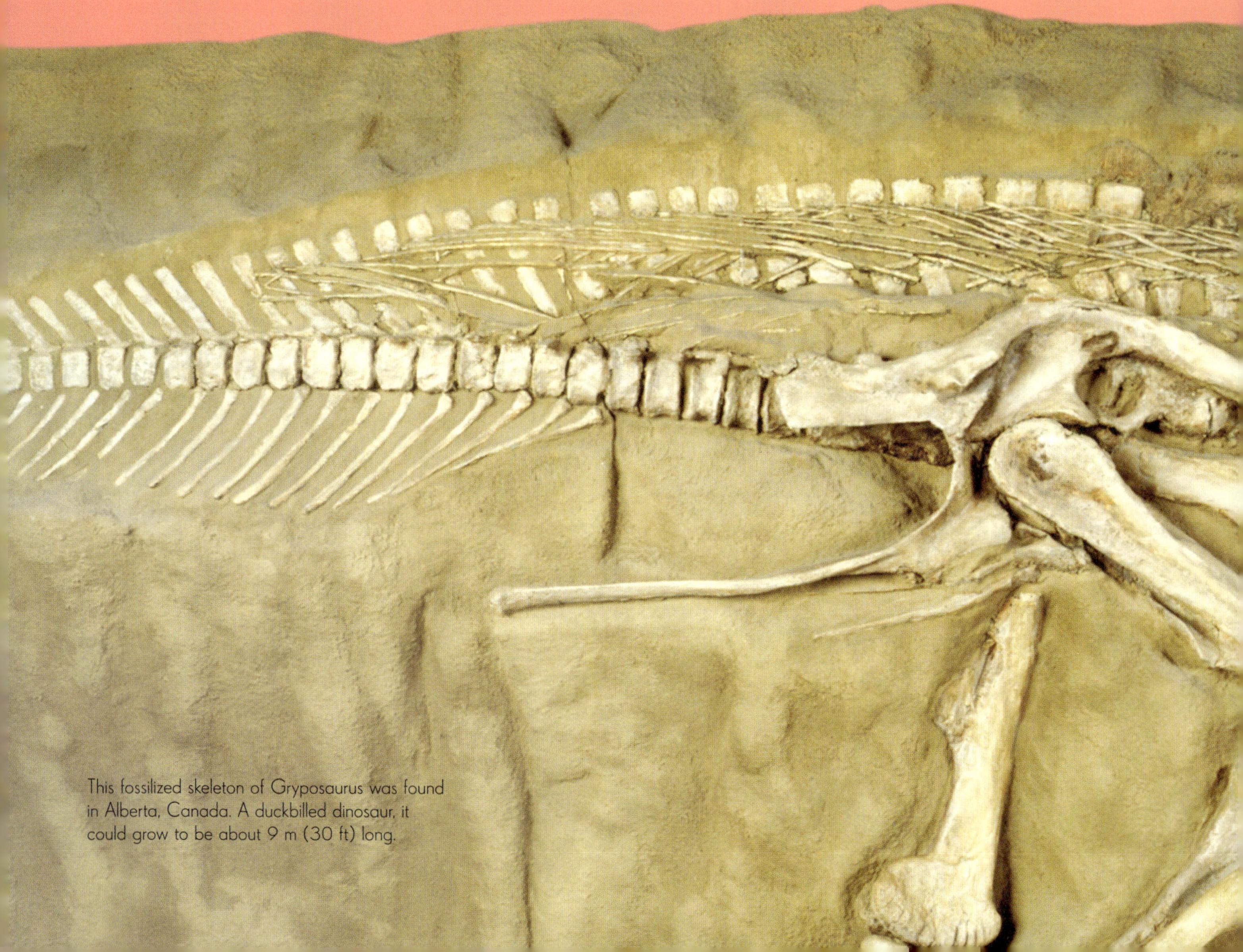
This fossilized skeleton of Gryposaurus was found in Alberta, Canada. A duckbilled dinosaur, it could grow to be about 9 m (30 ft) long.

The word "fossil" comes from the Latin word meaning "unearthed".

Buried in the earth, fossils are the ancient traces of plants and animals. They are made when the hard parts of a dead animal are replaced by minerals and become rock. Most fossils are millions of years old and are found in sedimentary rock.

This fossilized skeleton is of the dinosaur Gryposaurus. Fossil experts, called palaeontologists, have pieced together the skeleton so that we can see a complete picture of what the dinosaur would have looked like. For instance, the way the bones fit together tells us that the tail was held straight out and high up off the ground.

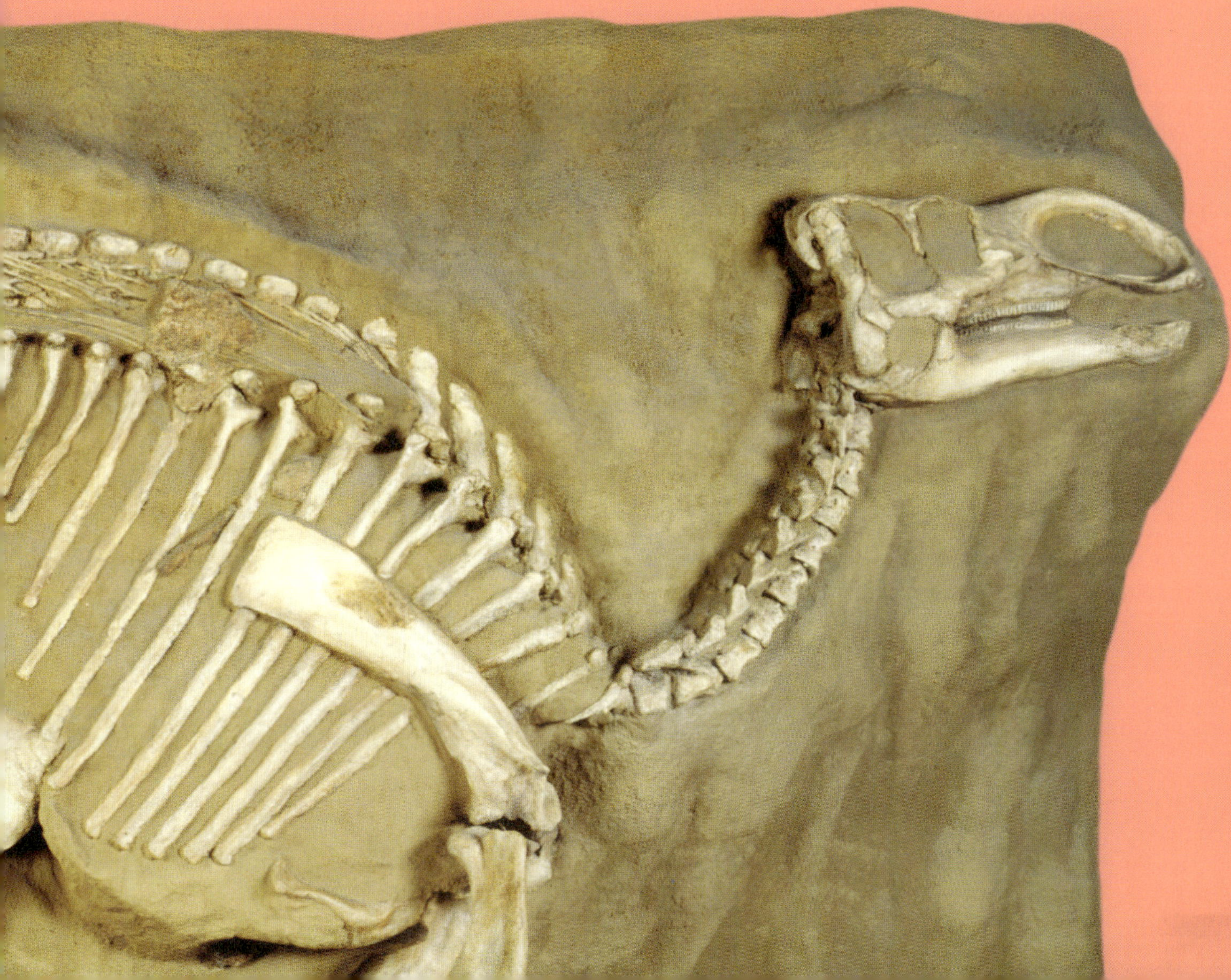

The word "marble" comes from the ancient Greek for "shining stone".

Marble

Migmatite

Schist

Skarn

Many types of metamorphic rock have stripy patterns because they're stretched and squeezed underground.

The enchanting Marble Caves of Chile lie on the shores of General Carrera Lake. Over thousands of years, the rock was dissolved and shaped by wind and water, resulting in a stunning maze of caves, tunnels, and columns.

Rocks – like marble – that are changed by heat or pressure underground are called metamorphic rocks. The name is from the ancient Greek words *meta*, which means "change", and *morph*, meaning "shape". Marble is formed from limestone, and it often has swirls running through it that are created by different coloured minerals in the rock. The natural beauty of marble has made it a favourite with artists and architects around the world.

The marble appears blue because it reflects the lake's shimmering turquoise waters.

These silver curls are from the Ore Mountains of Germany.

Metals

For thousands of years, valuable metals, such as gold, silver, and copper, have been discovered and mined from the surface layers of Earth. Usually, the metal is found as tiny pieces – in rocks called ores. Metals are often heated, melted, and mixed together to make them stronger. The mixes are called alloys. One of the first to be made was an alloy of copper and tin, called bronze.

Metalworkers hammer gleaming metals to turn them into household objects, like plates and cutlery, and to create beautiful jewellery. As pure silver is so delicate, it is often mixed with copper to make sterling silver, which is stronger. Gold, meanwhile, does not tarnish so easily and is valued for its soft, yellow sheen.

This piece of gold was found in Queensland, Australia.

Gold can be found as grains in river gravel. It is taken out by panning – water is swirled in a pan to wash away any lighter gravel, leaving the gold.

This copper is from Michigan, USA.

Copper is one of the oldest metals used by humans – dating back to about 10,000 years ago.

Carbon cycle

Carbon is central to life on Earth. It is found everywhere. It is in us and in every other living thing. Carbon is also found in some non-living things, such as fossil fuels (coal, oil, and gas) and certain rocks. The movement of carbon on Earth is called the carbon cycle.

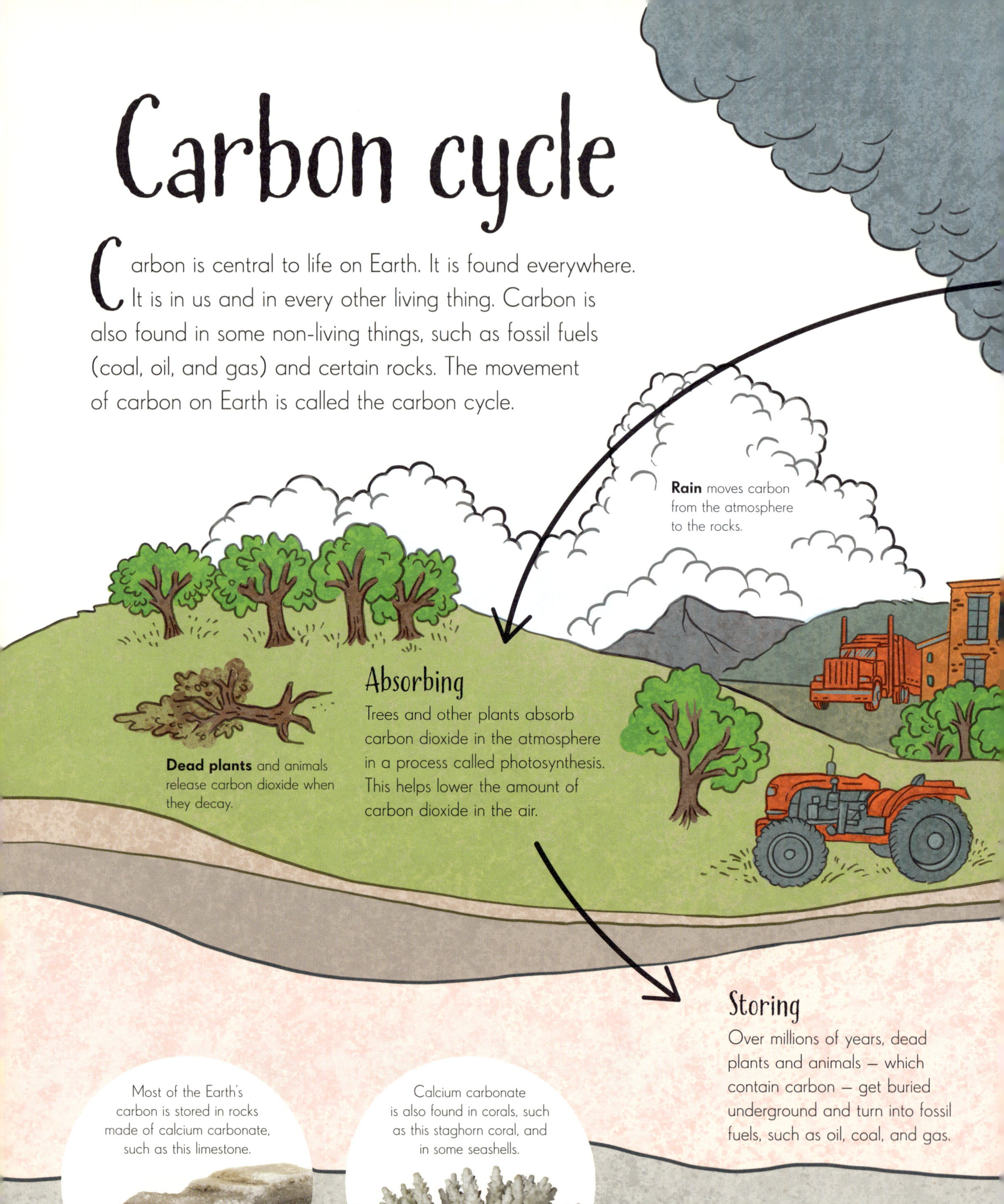

Rain moves carbon from the atmosphere to the rocks.

Dead plants and animals release carbon dioxide when they decay.

Absorbing

Trees and other plants absorb carbon dioxide in the atmosphere in a process called photosynthesis. This helps lower the amount of carbon dioxide in the air.

Storing

Over millions of years, dead plants and animals – which contain carbon – get buried underground and turn into fossil fuels, such as oil, coal, and gas.

Most of the Earth's carbon is stored in rocks made of calcium carbonate, such as this limestone.

Calcium carbonate is also found in corals, such as this staghorn coral, and in some seashells.

The Sun produces light energy, which plants use to absorb carbon dioxide during photosynthesis.

In the atmosphere

When we burn fossil fuels, the carbon is returned to the atmosphere and combines with oxygen in the air to make carbon dioxide (CO_2).

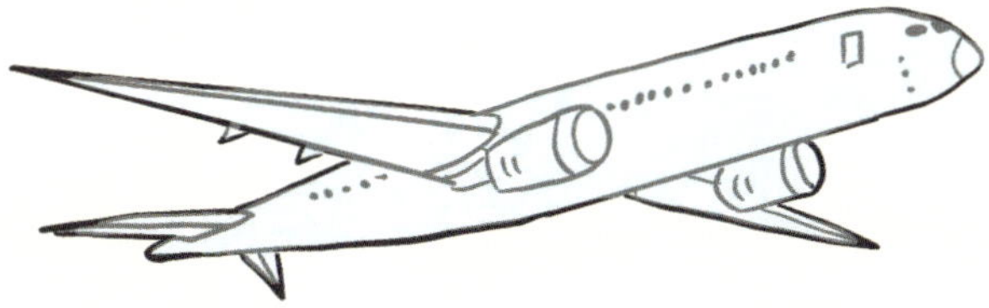

Releasing

Animals and other organisms expel carbon dioxide when they breathe out. When volcanoes erupt, they also return carbon to the atmosphere.

Oil rigs drill deep down under the ocean to extract oil and natural gas, which contain carbon.

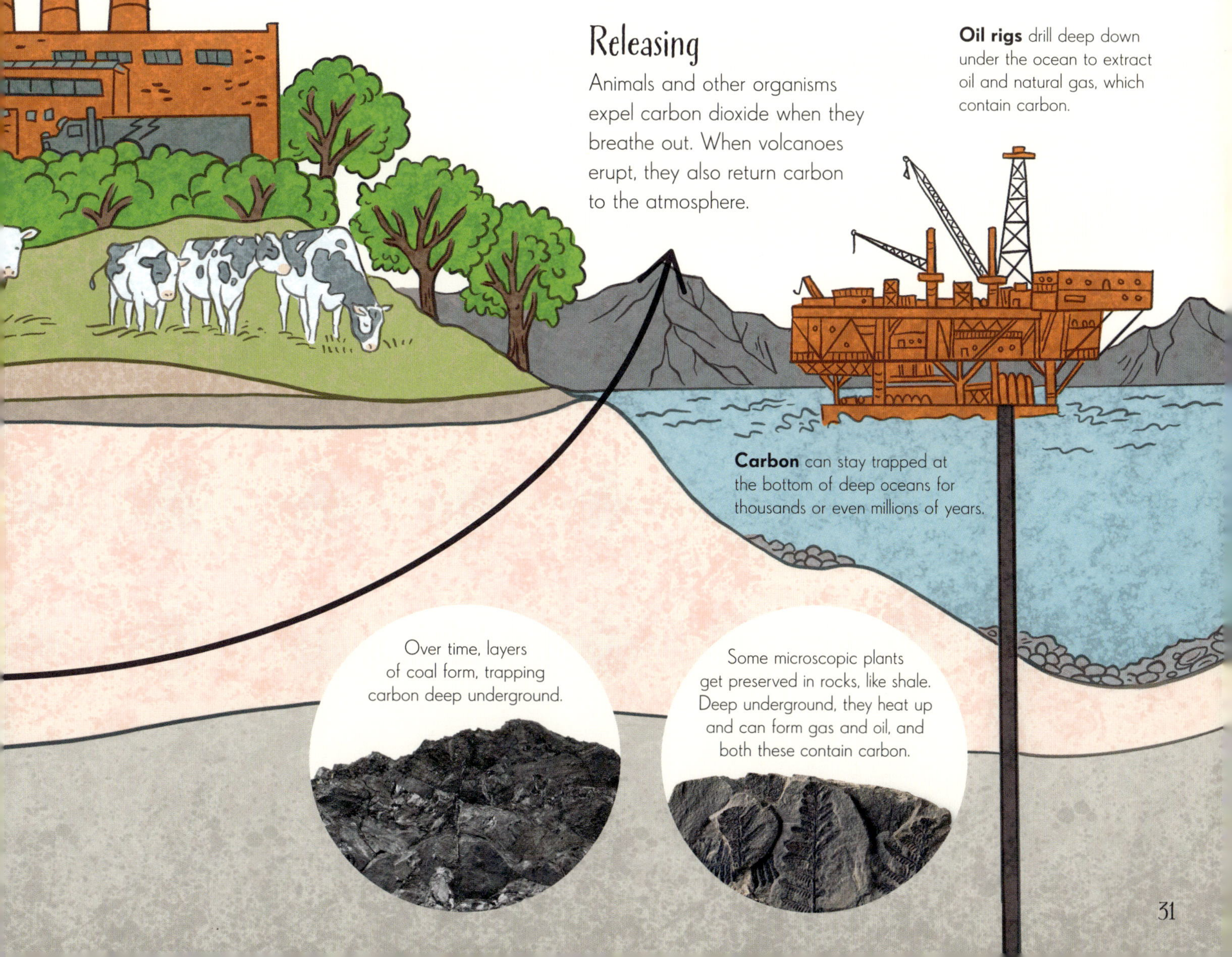

Carbon can stay trapped at the bottom of deep oceans for thousands or even millions of years.

Over time, layers of coal form, trapping carbon deep underground.

Some microscopic plants get preserved in rocks, like shale. Deep underground, they heat up and can form gas and oil, and both these contain carbon.

This dark purple amethyst comes from Uruguay.

Many amethysts were formed millions of years ago in volcanic rock.

Amethyst

In some rocks, gassy bubbles fill with fluid ingredients that slowly make crystals, including amethyst. The bubble becomes a crystal geode.

When you look at a crystal, such as this purple amethyst, you feel that nature is putting on its best, most dazzling display. A crystal is a mineral that forms a shape with straight, flat sides called faces.

Purple amethyst belongs to the quartz family, whose other members include yellow citrine, grey smoky quartz, and pink rose quartz. Amethyst crystals can grow in gas bubbles called geodes. The gas bubbles form when molten lava cools and then sets solid. Crystals then grow layer by layer from the edge of the bubble towards the middle. They can take thousands or even millions of years to form.

Diamond

Beautiful and valuable, diamonds may look fragile but they are actually the hardest natural minerals in the world. The word "diamond" comes from an ancient Greek term meaning "indestructible", and it is true that it is almost impossible to destroy a diamond.

Diamonds score a perfect 10 on the Mohs hardness scale for minerals. This means they cannot be scratched by any other mineral, apart from another diamond. They can, however, scratch all other minerals. This includes emeralds, which score 7.5–8 on the Mohs scale, and rubies and sapphires, at 9. Diamonds are often cut and polished to make gemstones. A diamond-cutter will cut flat sides, called facets, and polish the diamond. The size and shape of each facet is carefully worked out to make the diamond sparkle.

Uncut diamond

Diamonds are so hard they can be used in powerful drills to cut stone and metal.

Cut diamond

Emerald

Ruby

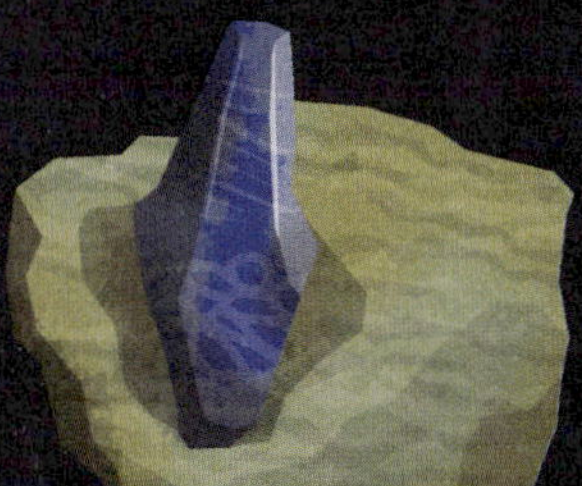

Sapphire

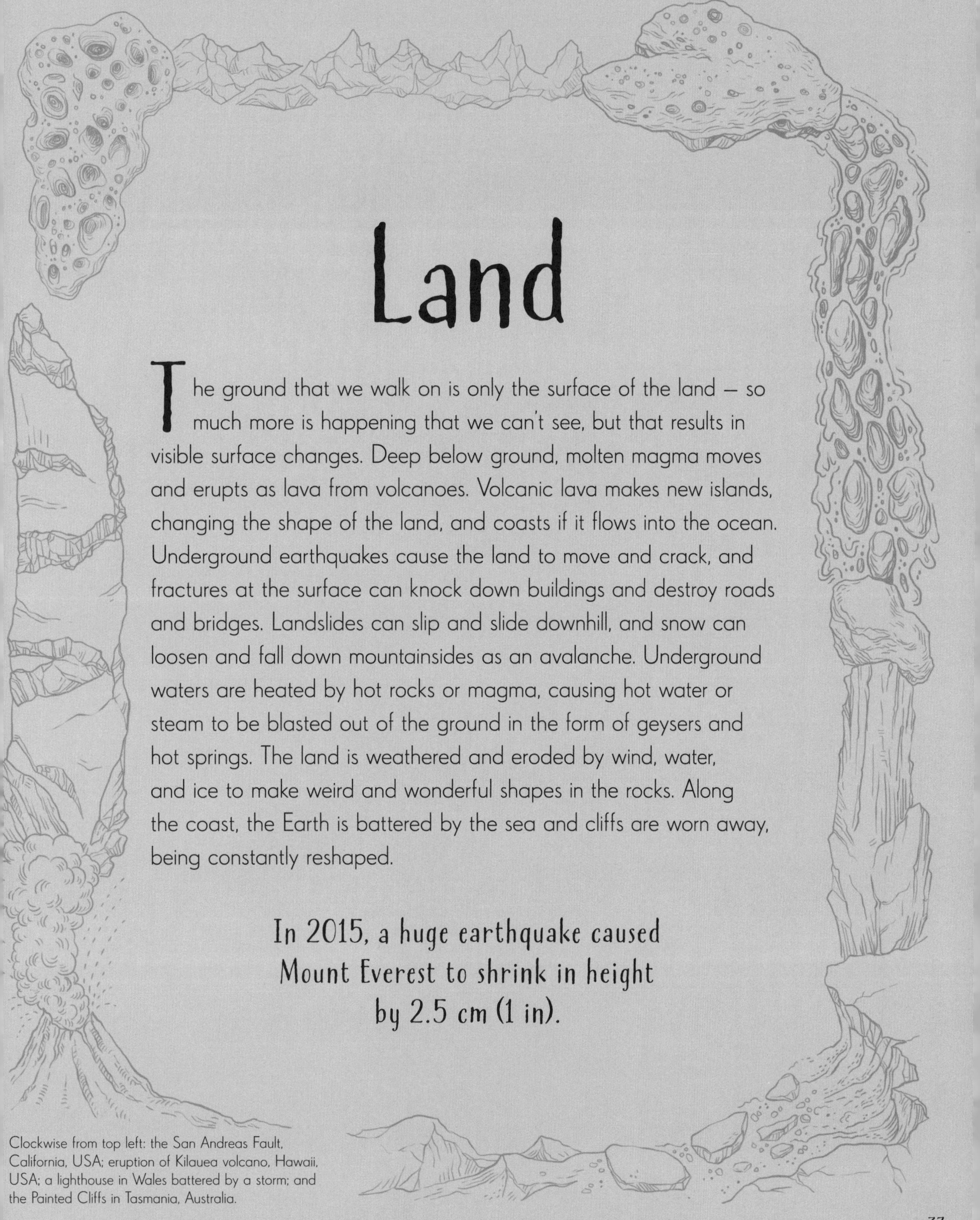

Land

The ground that we walk on is only the surface of the land – so much more is happening that we can't see, but that results in visible surface changes. Deep below ground, molten magma moves and erupts as lava from volcanoes. Volcanic lava makes new islands, changing the shape of the land, and coasts if it flows into the ocean. Underground earthquakes cause the land to move and crack, and fractures at the surface can knock down buildings and destroy roads and bridges. Landslides can slip and slide downhill, and snow can loosen and fall down mountainsides as an avalanche. Underground waters are heated by hot rocks or magma, causing hot water or steam to be blasted out of the ground in the form of geysers and hot springs. The land is weathered and eroded by wind, water, and ice to make weird and wonderful shapes in the rocks. Along the coast, the Earth is battered by the sea and cliffs are worn away, being constantly reshaped.

In 2015, a huge earthquake caused Mount Everest to shrink in height by 2.5 cm (1 in).

Clockwise from top left: the San Andreas Fault, California, USA; eruption of Kilauea volcano, Hawaii, USA; a lighthouse in Wales battered by a storm; and the Painted Cliffs in Tasmania, Australia.

Earth's plates

Tectonic plates are the jigsaw-puzzle pieces of Earth's outer shell. The pieces are constantly moving, changing Earth's surface. Scientists study the shifting plates to better understand how continents, oceans, mountains, volcanoes, and other features of Earth are formed.

Timeline

The continents we see today have not always looked like this. Plates move relative to each other at different rates, from 2–15 cm (1–6 in) per year.

225 million years ago

A supercontinent called Pangaea began to break up into pieces.

200 million years ago

Two continents formed, and these too began to break up.

65 million years ago | **Present day** | **50 million years in the future**

You can start to recognize the main continents and oceans, even as they continue to move.

The continents as they are today were roughly in place about 20 million years ago.

In the future, as Africa moves further north, the Mediterranean will close up.

Between two plates

Also known as the "Island of Ice and Fire", Iceland is blessed with glaciers, active volcanoes, natural hot springs, waterfalls, and valleys. This island's extraordinary landscape is due to its unusual position on Earth.

Iceland sits in the middle of the Atlantic Ocean between two tectonic plates – the North American Plate and the Eurasian Plate. Between these lies the Mid-Atlantic Ridge – a part of the Mid-Oceanic Ridge that runs down the middle of the Atlantic Ocean, forming the longest mountain range in the world. While most of the ridge is underwater, sometimes it surfaces as land. This is because millions of years ago, underwater volcanoes erupted, causing hot, liquid magma to rise up, spread out, and create islands, including the island of Iceland.

The two tectonic plates are moving apart at a rate of about 2.5 cm (1 in) per year.

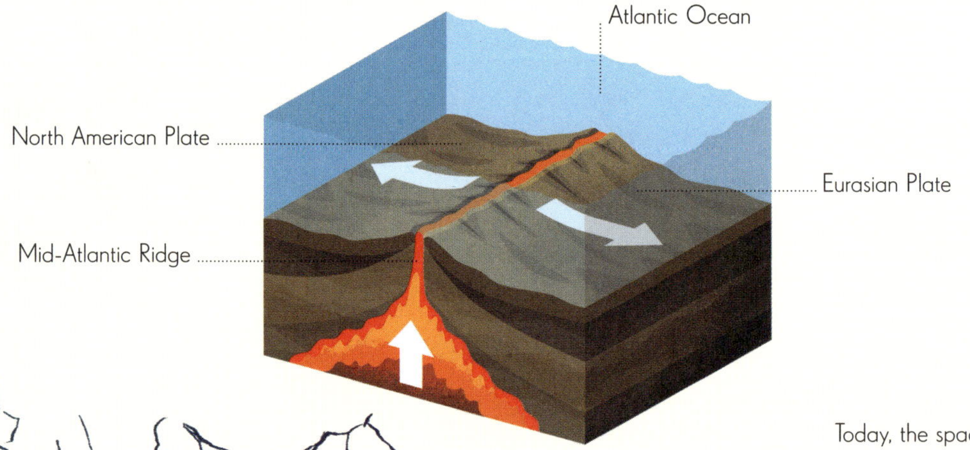

Today, the space between the two tectonic plates along the Almannagjá rift valley in Iceland is partly covered with water.

Forming the boundary between two of Earth's tectonic plates, the San Andreas Fault has caused huge earthquakes in the USA.

Fault line

The Pacific Plate and the North American Plate slide past each other along the plate boundary in California.

The plate movement has caused frequent and sometimes powerful earthquakes over millions of years.

There are about half a million earthquakes in the world each year, but they are usually too deep underground or too minor for us to feel. Most earthquakes happen at the boundary, or fault line, where two tectonic plates move past one another. If the edges of moving plates get stuck against each other, pressure builds up. Eventually, the pressure becomes so great that the plates judder on, causing a violent earthquake.

From space, the San Andreas Fault in California, USA, can be seen as a scar on the land, but it also carries on deep into the ground. In 1906, the fault line caused the great earthquake of San Francisco, which destroyed the city and killed more than 3,000 people.

The San Andreas Fault extends about 1,200 km (746 miles) across California.

Rising mountains

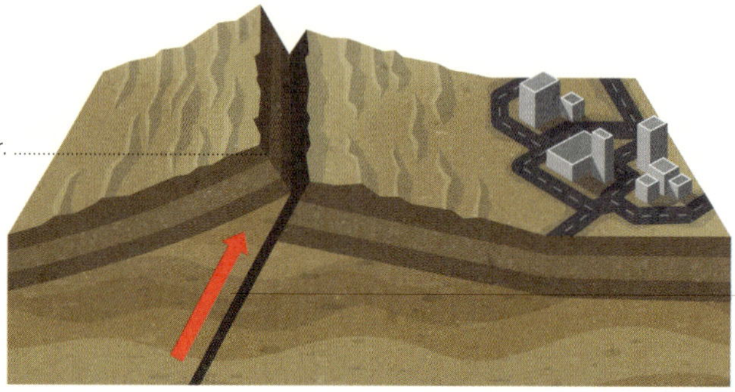

Fault blocks in the Earth's crust move up over each other.

Mount Whitney is the highest mountain in Sierra Nevada, at 4,418 m (14,494 ft) above sea level.

The Sierra Nevada range is growing by about 1 mm (0.04 in) a year.

Mountains are not fixed in place – they move, though very, very slowly. Over millions of years, mountains have been pushed upwards as the land folds and moves together. This can happen at the edges of blocks of the Earth's crust called tectonic plates.

The Sierra Nevada mountains in California, USA, are fault-block mountains. This means that one block of land has been pushed up over another block and the risen land has created a mountain. Most of the large fault blocks formed 5–10 million years ago. And they've been making mountains ever since.

Mountains form when the Earth's crust bends and buckles.

Folding rock

About 20 per cent of Earth's land is mountainous.

Because of movement in the Earth's crust over millions of years, a mountain may form. The most common type is a fold mountain. Where tectonic plates meet, the plates can collide and squash together creating folds in the rocks. The folds can be small, affecting even just a hand-sized rock, or they can be huge and make up entire mountain ranges, such as the Himalayas in Asia. The patterns vary, too – some make curving "S" shapes, while others might zig-zag from side to side..

While not as massive as the Himalayas, the limestone cliffs on the Greek island of Crete are perhaps just as amazing. Here, the layers of rocks have been folded into striking "V" shapes, or chevron folds. The folds are straight and bend sharply at one point, called the hinge zone.

Here you can see chevron folds in the limestone cliffs on the Greek island of Crete.

Some people believe that the Goddess of Salt Mountain gives out positive energy and aids healing.

Salt dome

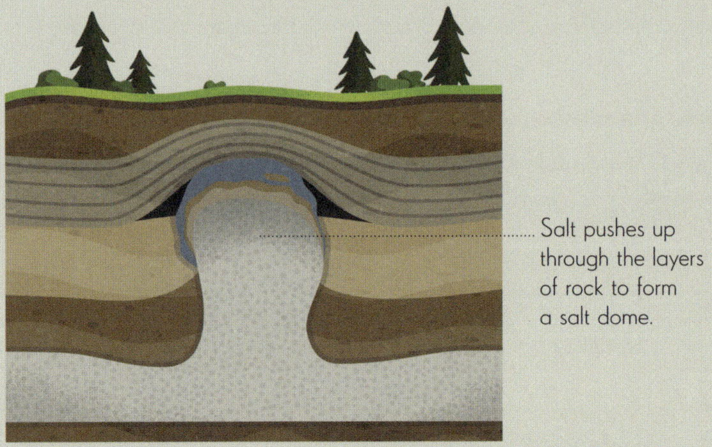

The Goddess of Salt Mountain is on Hormuz Island in the Persian Gulf.

The Iranian island of Hormuz glows with red, orange, and yellow rock because of the many minerals that are found there. And out of these colourful hues looms the most extraordinary sight of all – the Goddess of Salt Mountain. This stunning "mountain" is in fact a salt dome.

A salt dome is a mound formed when salt rises up into other rocks causing a unique formation. As tectonic plates break apart to make new ocean, or collide to close an ocean, the depth of the sea water changes. When shallow seas dry out, the salt is left behind. If this happens again and again over millions of years, the salt gets thicker, layer by layer. The salt can become buried and pressed down by the layers of rock above it. Eventually, this pressure from above means the salt gets squeezed up towards the surface, to make a salt dome.

Child of Krakatau

Explosive volcanoes like Anak Krakatau have thick, sticky lava and steep sides. This type of volcano, with its layers of lava and ash, is called a stratovolcano.

When the Indonesian volcano Krakatau erupted in 1883, it was so loud, it was heard across the ocean in Australia. It was one of the most destructive volcanic explosions in history. After this cataclysmic event, all that was left was a huge caldera. From this, a new, smaller volcano emerged – Anak Krakatau, whose name means "child of Krakatau". In 2018, it erupted and caused a devastating tsunami, with waves that travelled far inland. Anak Krakatau is an active volcano, and is still erupting today.

When Anak Krakatau erupted in 2018 it caused tsunami waves around 5 m (16 ft) high.

Anak Krakatau is a small volcano that formed in the caldera of Krakatau.

Ash cloud

Bombs are bigger than 64 mm (2.5 in)

Lapilli are between 2 mm–64 mm (0.08 in–2.5 in) in size.

Volcanic dust is less than 2 mm (0.08 in) in size.

When a volcano erupts violently it can throw out an ash cloud, wreaking havoc in the atmosphere. It can block out the Sun, make the air smelly, and can also disrupt air travel. If volcanic ash gets into an aircraft engine it can cause it to fail. This is what happened in 2010 when a volcano in Iceland called Eyjafjallajökull erupted, causing thousands of flights to be cancelled.

An ash cloud is made up of small shattered fragments of rock. As well as erupting lava and ash, explosive volcanoes can throw out rocks of varying sizes. These are known as pyroclasts. The types of pyroclasts have different names, depending on their size. Bombs, or blocks, can be made from solid magma shaped like a rugby ball. Other types include tiny rounded fragments called lapilli, and volcanic dust, which can be scratchy with sharp glassy bits in it.

Ash clouds can rise as high as 40 km (25 miles) into the sky.

Santa Maria Volcano, in Guatemala, has been actively erupting since 1922. At the end of February 2023, the ash cloud rose 700 m (2,300 ft) above the summit.

The temperature of red-hot pahoehoe lava is at least 600°C (1,112°F).

Pahoehoe lava

It can take years for a lava flow to cool and solidify as rock.

The red-hot, runny lava that erupts from volcanoes is called pahoehoe, from the Hawaiian word meaning "swirling". It is pronounced "pa-ho-ee-ho-ee", which even sounds swirly when you say it out loud! The other, not so interesting, name for it is ropey lava.

The surface of pahoehoe lava is often smooth, though sometimes it can be wrinkled like the skin of an elephant. When it flows, it moves quite slowly – you can probably walk faster. It comes oozing out of the Earth's crust as it cools, rather like toothpaste being squeezed out of a tube. As the lava cools further, it turns black and hard, first at the surface and then deeper down. And it is this that makes the ropey texture – the hot lava inside crinkles up the cooler and harder outer crust. The red-hot lava also takes longer to cool. It is so hot, you could cook an egg on it.

Pahoehoe lava flows create amazing patterns that look like twisted rope.

A'a lava

On the island of Hawaii in the Pacific Ocean, scorching molten rock is pouring out of Kilauea, one of the island's five volcanoes. A'a (pronounced "ah-ah") lava flows fast, in bright orange streams called channels. The lava is very runny and can sometimes flow at a rate of around 50 kph (30 mph). This is about the average speed of a car – and much, much faster than you can run.

The name "a'a" means "rough, stony lava" in Hawaiian. This is because this lava cools as sharp, chunky rock. As it cools, it forms a crust of black basalt rock, which gets broken up as it flows. The rock becomes hard and sharp, making it difficult to walk over.

Kilauea is the most active of Hawaii's five volcanoes.

This bright orange a'a lava channel is flowing out of the Kilauea volcano in Hawaii. A'a lava can flow for more than 100 km (60 miles).

Acid pools

The vibrant and colourful hot springs of Dallol may look dazzling, but looks can be deceiving. Sitting within a volcanic plain in Ethiopia, these springs are very dangerous – the water is hot and acidic, and it can burn you.

Just below the surface of the Earth's crust, a sea of red-hot, molten rock, called magma, radiates heat all around, like a saturated sponge. Rain and seawater trickle down underground, making their way through cracks in the Earth's crust, and are heated by the magma below. This causes the hot water, now full of minerals such as sulphur, potash, and iron, to rise up and spill out onto the surface of the Earth. Some of the minerals dissolve in the water, creating bright green pools of pure acid.

The hot spring water of Dallol can reach temperatures of 100°C (212°F).

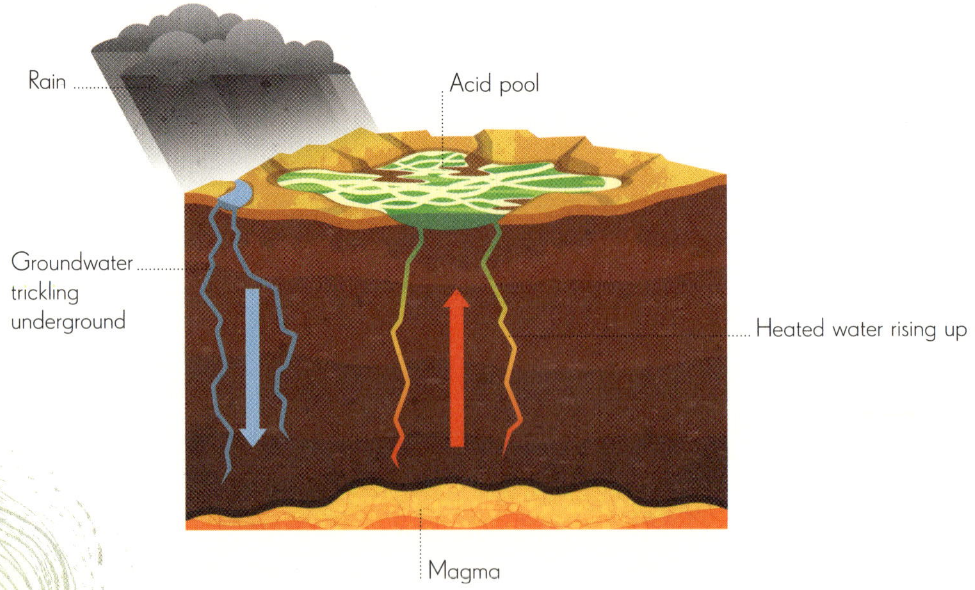

The heated water often evaporates in the Sun, leaving behind stepped walls called terraces.

Strokkur geyser is in the Haukadalur valley in Iceland, an area known for geysers and other geothermal features such as mud pools and fumaroles.

The water in a geyser can be three times hotter than boiling water.

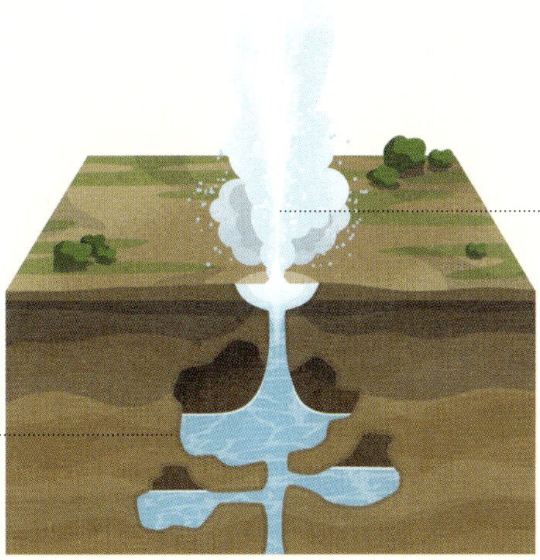

Geyser

You don't have to wait very long to see the Strokkur geyser in Iceland erupt. It does so every 6–10 minutes. It usually erupts 15–20 m (49–66 ft) into the air, although it can sometimes reach twice that height. It's a stunning sight to behold. Don't get too close though, as it spurts boiling water and lets off superheated steam.

When water makes its way deep underground it can get heated up by hot magma. The magma heats the rocks, which heat the water until the pressure is so great that there is a hydrothermal explosion and the geyser erupts.

Barrier island

As their name suggests, barrier islands protect nearby coastlines. These islands are formed by the tides. Waves repeatedly deposit sediment, which builds up over time to form land.

North Carolina, USA, has nearly 20 barrier islands along its coastline. They protect the mainland from the ocean waves.

Islands

An island is a piece of land that is surrounded by water and is smaller than a continent. Islands can vary from rocky outcrops that can form in a lake or a river to larger stretches of land found in seas and oceans. Islands develop in different ways, and here are the main types.

Tidal island

This type of island depends on the tides. Usually it is connected to the mainland, but at high tide it gets cut off by the sea and becomes an island.

At low tide, you can walk to Mont-Saint-Michel in Normandy, France. At high tide, it becomes an island in a bay.

Hawaii, USA, is a group of islands formed from five volcanoes, and Mauna Loa is the largest.

Volcanic island

Many volcanoes erupt from the sea floor, and some grow so big they create an island! The islands of Hawaii have built up from so much volcanic lava that they are now up to 9,700 m (32,000 ft) above the ocean floor.

Continental islands

Most of the largest islands are continental islands – they have become separated from the rest of the mainland continent. This may happen because of rising sea levels or the movement of tectonic plates. The island of Madagascar, for example, was once joined to the Indian subcontinent and now lies off the coast of Africa.

Madagascar has a different climate and ecosystem to the rest of Africa and is home to unique wildlife.

How Madagascar formed

170 million years ago
Long before Madagascar was an island, one supercontinent existed: Pangaea. This began breaking into smaller pieces of land.

135 million years ago Madagascar was on the edge of one landmass, which was to become the Indian subcontinent.

88 million years ago Madagascar split off from the Indian subcontinent and started to move towards Africa.

Coral island

Corals are sea animals with hard skeletons. Gradually, fragments of the skeletons can build up on top of a coral reef to create an island. Coral islands are usually found in tropical areas and have sandy beaches covered with palm trees.

The Maldives in the Indian Ocean is made up of a chain of coral islands.

When measured from the ocean floor, Mauna Kea volcano on the island of Hawaii is the tallest mountain on Earth, at 9,760 m (32,000 ft) high.

When an underwater volcano erupts, the lava solidifies and builds up in a cone shape. Eventually, an island may emerge above the surface.

Volcanic island

Volcanoes can form at plate boundaries, when melted rock in the Earth's mantle breaks through the crust as the plates move apart. This can even happen under the sea. If a volcano erupts from the ocean floor and reaches the surface, an island may form.

The Azores are a group of volcanic islands in the Atlantic Ocean. They sit at the junction of three tectonic plates – North American, Eurasian, and African. About 8 million years ago, the lava built up so high that it reached the ocean's surface and the islands began to take shape. Crater lakes are a feature of São Miguel, one of the island in the Azores. A crater lake is formed from an ancient submerged volcano – the water sits within the volcano's crater at sea level. Here, natural circular swimming pools can form, with their clear waters warm enough to swim in all year round.

This crater lake is part of the Vila Franca do Campo islet, near São Miguel island in the Atlantic Ocean.

Sea stacks

Waves bash against soft rock.

The rock starts to erode.

Over time an arch may form.

The arch collapses, leaving the stack.

The Twelve Apostle sea stacks reach up to 45 m (150 ft) in height.

Our coastlines are not fixed. Constant battering by waves, rain, and ice slowly wears away rock. This is called erosion. Storm waves on the beach have enough energy to lift even large boulders, and bash them against cliffs. Over time, the shape of the shoreline changes, forming caves and arches. And if the roof of a rock arch gets completely eroded, it collapses, leaving behind a rock pillar, called a stack, in the ocean.

The powerful pounding waves of the Southern Ocean have carved out a unique group of sea stacks off the coast of southern Australia, called the Twelve Apostles. Despite their name, only eight stacks have ever been seen, though more may form in the future as the waves continue to crash onto the shore.

The Twelve Apostles in Port Campbell National Park, Victoria, Australia, is a collection of sea stacks made from soft limestone.

Shaping stone

Earth's landscape is constantly changing – this can happen quickly after a storm or a flood or more slowly, over millions of years. So if you could journey back through time, you might see how mountains are worn down, little by little, and how rocks are broken down by the weather into smaller pieces, then blown by the wind or washed away.

Wind on its own wouldn't do much damage. But if the wind carries dust or sand grains, they act like ammunition. They bash against the rock and wear it away. In places like Antelope Canyon – in a sandy desert in Arizona, USA – wonderful shapes have been carved out of the rock by wind and water. Here, fast-flowing flood waters carried sand and rocks that gradually sculpted natural passageways through the soft sandstone over a period of millions of years.

Antelope Canyon is a sacred place for the Navajo people of southwestern USA.

The canyon is dry and narrow with steep sides – and it can flood very quickly.

Sydney sandstone in Australia is about 235 million years old.

Honeycomb weathering

When rock is worn away and broken down by water, wind, or ice, this is called weathering, and one of the most extraordinary types is called honeycomb weathering. Here, lots of little pits appear in the rock that look like the honeycomb produced by bees in their hives.

Honeycomb weathering is found by the sea, in the desert, or even in Arctic regions. It is usually made by salty seawater and the wind. The wind helps dry the salt water on the rocks. Then, over time, the salt from the seawater makes salt crystals. As the crystals grow, they push into the rock, knock bits of it away, and make little holes that gradually become bigger.

This honeycomb pattern is on sandstone on the sea cliffs at Elgol beach on the Isle of Skye, Scotland.

The White Cliffs of Dover stretch for 13 km (8 miles) along the south coast of England.

Chalk cliffs

These are some of the fossils often found in chalk.

Bivalve

Echinoid

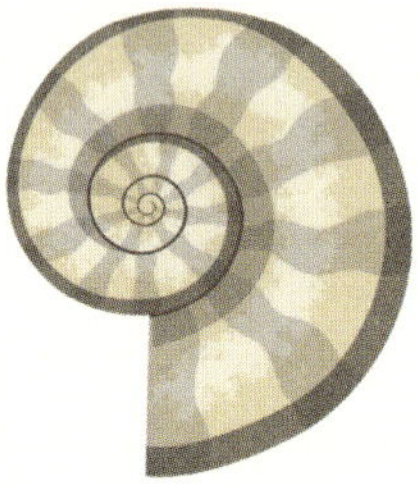

Ammonite

Cliffs are found where the rocks meet the sea along the coast. If you look back at cliffs from the beach or from out at sea, you can see the layers in the rocks, which tell you something about how the cliffs were made.

The White Cliffs of Dover form a stunning landmark along the south coast of England and they have their own unique story to tell. They are white because they are made from chalk. This soft rock is itself made from thousands of tiny skeletons of sea organisms and shells, crushed together over millions of years. Constant battering by the waves and tides wears away the crumbly chalk easily, often revealing ancient fossils wedged into the rock. Amazingly, these cliffs weren't always above water – in fact, they were once part of the seafloor! About 66–100 million years ago, the sea level sank and the chalk got pushed up, creating cliffs that soar into the sky.

On a clear day, the White Cliffs of Dover can be seen from the coast of France, just 32 km (20 miles) away on the other side of the English Channel.

Landslides can move at speeds of more than 55 kph (35 mph).

Landslide

The ground beneath our feet is usually solid rock or earth, but sometimes it can move. If the earth on a steep slope comes loose, it can slip out of place and thunder downhill with tremendous force. This is what we call a landslide.

Landslides might happen as a result of a juddering earthquake, but that's not their only cause. In tropical areas of the world, heavy rains can soak the soil, making it heavy and more likely to slip down a slope. Trees can help prevent this – their roots soak up the water and help to keep the ground firm and bound together. Not surprisingly, therefore, landslides are especially common in places where many trees have been cut down or burned. The soil there is more likely to flood, and even to tumble downhill as a destructive landslide.

Here you can see that both soil and trees have slipped down a mountain slope in Vorarlberg, Austria.

Avalanche

A single skier can cause enough vibrations to set off an avalanche.

When a mass of snow and ice suddenly crashes down the side of a mountain, it is called an avalanche – and it is extremely dangerous. The snow can rush downhill incredibly fast, reaching speeds of up to 320 kph (200 mph). Avalanches surge down steep mountainsides and into valleys, sweeping away rocks, trees, and anything else in their way. They can spread out like a thick, white blanket up to 1 km (0.5 mile) wide, and can even bury whole villages.

Avalanches can be caused by heavy snowfall, melting ice, strong winds, or earthquakes. They can even be created by humans and animals moving around on the slopes, or by loud noises. In 1916, during World War I, several avalanches in the Italian Alps were triggered by the firing of guns, and thousands of soldiers were killed.

This avalanche is speeding down a slope on Lhotse mountain in the Himalayas in Asia.

Water

When planet Earth formed, there was no water – the surface was just hot molten lava. Nothing could survive. It took millions of years before the Earth had cooled enough for water to form. Rain filled the seabeds, and salts from the crust beneath them made them salty. Rainwater on land filled rivers and lakes with freshwater.

Today, we see rivers rushing down steep hills where they wear away rock and make waterfalls and rapids. When the land is not so steep and the water spreads out, the land may flood. Out at sea, there are powerful waves, whirlpools, and storms. Deep beneath the waves, seafloor sediment piles up and underwater vents may release hot acids. Seawater freezes as sea ice, and glaciers form into icebergs. The frozen water and snow of glaciers gouge out valleys that may refill with seawater as deep fjords.

Without fresh water, there would be no plants or animals on Earth, and we could not survive. We wouldn't have the amazing variety of life on land or in the deep ocean waters.

Around 70 per cent of the Earth's surface is covered by oceans.

Clockwise from top: a colourful coral reef in the Red Sea, Egypt; a huge wave, Western Australia; Sasyk-Sivash red salt lake, Crimea, Russia; and a braided river, Alaska, USA.

Water cycle

We need water to survive. Without water, there would be no plants, and animals wouldn't survive either. Planet Earth is just the right temperature to hold water. For millions of years, water has moved between the sea, the air, and the land – this is the water cycle.

Heat from the Sun warms the surface of the sea.

Wind blows some clouds over land.

Moisture from plants

Plants suck up water through their roots, then release this into the atmosphere as water vapour, a process called transpiration. This adds moisture to the air and helps form more clouds.

Making clouds

As warm water vapour rises, it reaches higher, colder air and cools. When it is cool enough, the water vapour condenses, changing to liquid and forming clouds.

Rising from the sea

Over time, the surface of the sea warms up and some of the water evaporates. This means it rises up into the air as water vapour.

Water changes state in the water cycle. It can be a solid, liquid, or a gas.

Large **rain clouds** can look dark because when they are so thick they block out the Sun's light.

Rainfall

If clouds become thick with water vapour, eventually, water droplets fall from the clouds as rain or, when it's colder, as snow or hail.

Rivers run down to the sea.

Surface water

Water runs downhill, joining streams and rivers, where it eventually flows into the sea. Some water seeps into the soil and feeds plants or goes underground through cracks in rocks and ends up in the sea.

Braided rivers are fertile hotspots for a huge variety of birds, fish, and plant life.

Braided river

When the land is quite flat and wide, such as in a plain between mountains, a river has space to wander – winding, wiggling, and waggling as it goes. The river may even split into smaller rivers and streams, and so becomes what is called a braided river.

A braided river flows fast and then slow. It doesn't have enough energy to keep hold of the gravel, sand, and mud that it has been carrying, so it drops them as it makes its way through the land, creating hundreds of little islands. The sandy islands move and change as the river continues on its journey, splitting and joining again to make an everchanging pattern. It looks almost as if it has been painted onto the landscape.

Here you can see the blue patterning made by the small streams and channels of a braided river in Iceland.

River shapes

The steep, fast-flowing parts of a river are called rapids.

An oxbow lake forms when a bend in the river gets cut off.

A floodplain is a flat area of land beside a river.

Rivers always flow downhill, carrying water from the mountains and hills down to the sea. Where the mountains are steep, the river travels faster. Where the land is flatter, the river may slow down, spread out, and become much wider.

On their journey, rivers create different shapes in the landscape. If the water has to drop down over a cliff, it might make a waterfall. On flat land and flood plains, the river can change direction, curving or meandering as it goes. In some places it wiggles, while in others it snakes into "S" shapes or large loops called oxbows. Sometimes, an oxbow loop gets cut off from the river and becomes an oxbow lake, like the ones shown here in the Yukon Delta in Alaska, USA. They are also called horseshoe lakes – can you see why?

Once an oxbow lake is formed it becomes a stillwater lake and no water flows into or out of it.

The Yukon Delta in Alaska is one of the largest river deltas in the world.

The Ganges Delta is the world's largest river delta.

River delta

Flat and trianglular shaped, river deltas get their name from a letter of the Greek alphabet called delta, because the Greek letter is itself shaped like a triangle.

River deltas are huge, flat areas of sand and mud that have been deposited by a river. The sediment blocks the original course of the river, making it spill out into several small channels. Deltas, such as the Ganges Delta in India, have some of the most fertile soil in the world. The land is so good for farming because the rivers wash soil down from the mountains and hills and spread it out over the area when it floods. The Ganges water comes all the way from the Himalayas. More than 120 million people make their home on the Ganges Delta, and many farm the land, producing crops such as jute, rice, and tea.

The Ganges Delta empties into the Bay of Bengal.

Liquid Rainbow

The plant *Macarenia clavigera*, which is unique to Colombia, gives the river its brilliant pinky-red colour.

For most of the year, the waters of Caño Cristales, a fast-flowing river in the remote mountains of Colombia, run crystal clear over a shimmering, white riverbed. However, between the months of August and October, when the water is exactly the right depth, a magical transformation occurs and the river becomes a riot of colour.

From the rocky riverbed, vivid orange, green, and, especially, red aquatic plants suddenly burst into bloom. Set against the blue water and yellow sand, the plants create a dazzling display that has earned the Caño Cristales its nicknames of "Liquid Rainbow" and "River of Five Colours".

Macarenia clavigera has strong roots that hold on tightly to the rocky riverbed. This ensures that the plant doesn't get swept away, even when the water is flowing very fast.

Waterfall

Water falling over a cliff gradually wears it away, creating a waterfall. The softer rock layers in the cliff are worn away quicker than the harder rocks.

At Victoria Falls, water flows 108 m (355 ft) into the chasm below.

Thundering water crashing down from the mighty Victoria Falls is an awe-inspiring sight. This waterfall is on the border between Zambia and Zimbabwe in southern Africa. The local Lozi people call it *Mosi-oa-Tunya*, which means "the smoke that thunders". It is also known as "the place of a rainbow", because sunlight shining through the spray makes rainbows form.

Spray from the Falls is not only powerful and plentiful, it is useful, too. It helps water the surrounding dry landscape – allowing small rainforests to flourish, which provide a habitat for hundreds of plants and animals.

Right at the edge, on the top of Victoria Falls is "Devil's Pool" – amazingly, it is safe to swim in during the dry season when the currents aren't as strong.

Salt lake

Salt lakes can be deadly. Lake Natron in Tanzania contains natron – a salt that leaks into the water from the volcanic rock that surrounds it. This makes the water alkaline, like bleach.

Each time Lake Assal dries out, it leaves more salt, so the salt layers get thicker.

Lake Assal is 10 times saltier than the sea.

The lowest point on land in Africa and the third lowest on Earth, Lake Assal lies in Djibouti, 155 m (509 ft) below sea level. Most lakes are fed by freshwater rivers and streams, and have an outlet downstream. However, Lake Assal is a salt lake. It doesn't have an outlet and can only lose its water through evaporation, when the heat from the Sun makes moisture rise into the air. If the salt lake dries out altogether, it leaves a dry lake called a player, or salt flat.

Why is the water so salty? It is in fact fed by sea water from the Gulf of Aden nearby. It is warm, too, because it travels through geothermal springs, powered by underground warmth in the Earth's crust.

Crater Lake

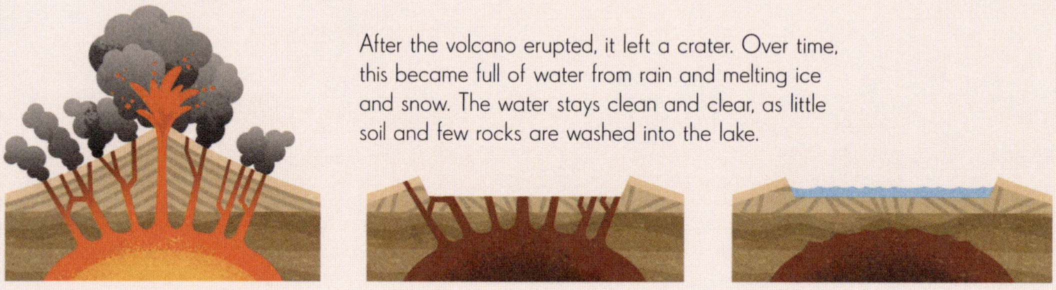

After the volcano erupted, it left a crater. Over time, this became full of water from rain and melting ice and snow. The water stays clean and clear, as little soil and few rocks are washed into the lake.

Crater Lake has an average depth of 350 m (1,148 ft).

Filled with pure, crystal-clear water, the deepest freshwater lake in the USA is a big, round basin called Crater Lake. This lake was formed about 7,700 years ago when Mount Mazama volcano erupted. The top of the volcano was blown off and the mountain was destroyed, leaving a crater, which filled with rain and snow.

Smaller eruptions continued for a few hundred years and made a little volcanic island in the lake called Wizard Island. There are no rivers flowing into or out of Crater Lake, but the sparkling clear water is continually refreshed by heavy rain and snowfall.

Crater Lake sits within an arc of volcanic mountains called the Cascades Volcanoes in western North America.

There are more than 1,000 fjords in Norway.

Fjord

As a glacier melts, it wears away the land, carving out a valley.

As the sea level rises, the water fills the valley and makes the fjord.

Fjords are flooded valleys made by the frozen ice of glaciers. The valleys are narrow, steep-sided, and very deep. During the last Ice Age, about 14,000 years ago, Norway was covered in glaciers. When the ice melted and the sea level rose, the sea filled the valleys and made the fjords that Norway is famous for, including the magnificent Geirangerfjord.

If fjords were without water, you would see that the bottoms of glacial valleys are U-shaped. This shape is made by the slow movement of the glaciers as they make their way down from the mountains to the sea, wearing away the ground beneath them as they go. Ice on its own won't wear away rock, but the glaciers pick up rocks as they move downhill and these grind away the earth and carve out valleys.

Geirangerfjord in Norway is more than 15 km (9 miles) long.

Hang Son Doong Cave is so wide, a jumbo jet could fly through it without its wings touching the sides.

Giant cave

Hang Son Doong Cave is more than 9 km (5.5 miles) long and 150 m (490 ft) wide.

The largest cave in the world was discovered by accident in 1991 by a local Vietnamese man called Ho Khanh while he was searching for timber. He didn't realize its significance at first, and soon forgot all about it. Nearly 20 years later, he met members of a caving expedition and he eventually led them back to what later became called Hang Son Doong Cave.

This vast cave features two hollow basins, called dolines, caused when parts of the roof collapsed. The dolines allow sunlight in, so that underground rainforests have flourished deep inside, watered by a fast-flowing underground river. The cave has a barrier wall made from calcite that is 90 m (295 ft) high called the Great Wall of Vietnam.

Hang Son Doong Cave is in Phong Nha-Ke Bang National Park, Vietnam.

The tallest stalagmite is in Zhi Jin Cave, in China, and is 70 m (230 ft) high.

Speleothems

Weird and wonderful rock formations called speleothems are found in some caves, especially those made from soft limestone. The name "speleothem" is from ancient Greek – *spelaion* means "cave", and *thema* means "deposit". When water drips down inside a limestone cave, it leaves behind minerals, such as calcite or aragonite. These build up very, very slowly – over thousands or even millions of years – to eventually form amazing shapes.

There are more than 300 different types of speleothem. Among the most common are spiky stalactites, which hang down from the ceiling. Depending on their shape, they are called different things, such as "straws" and "broomsticks". There are also more rounded stalagmites, which grow up from the floor of the cave.

These hanging stalactites and rising stalagmites are in Drach caves on the island of Mallorca, Spain.

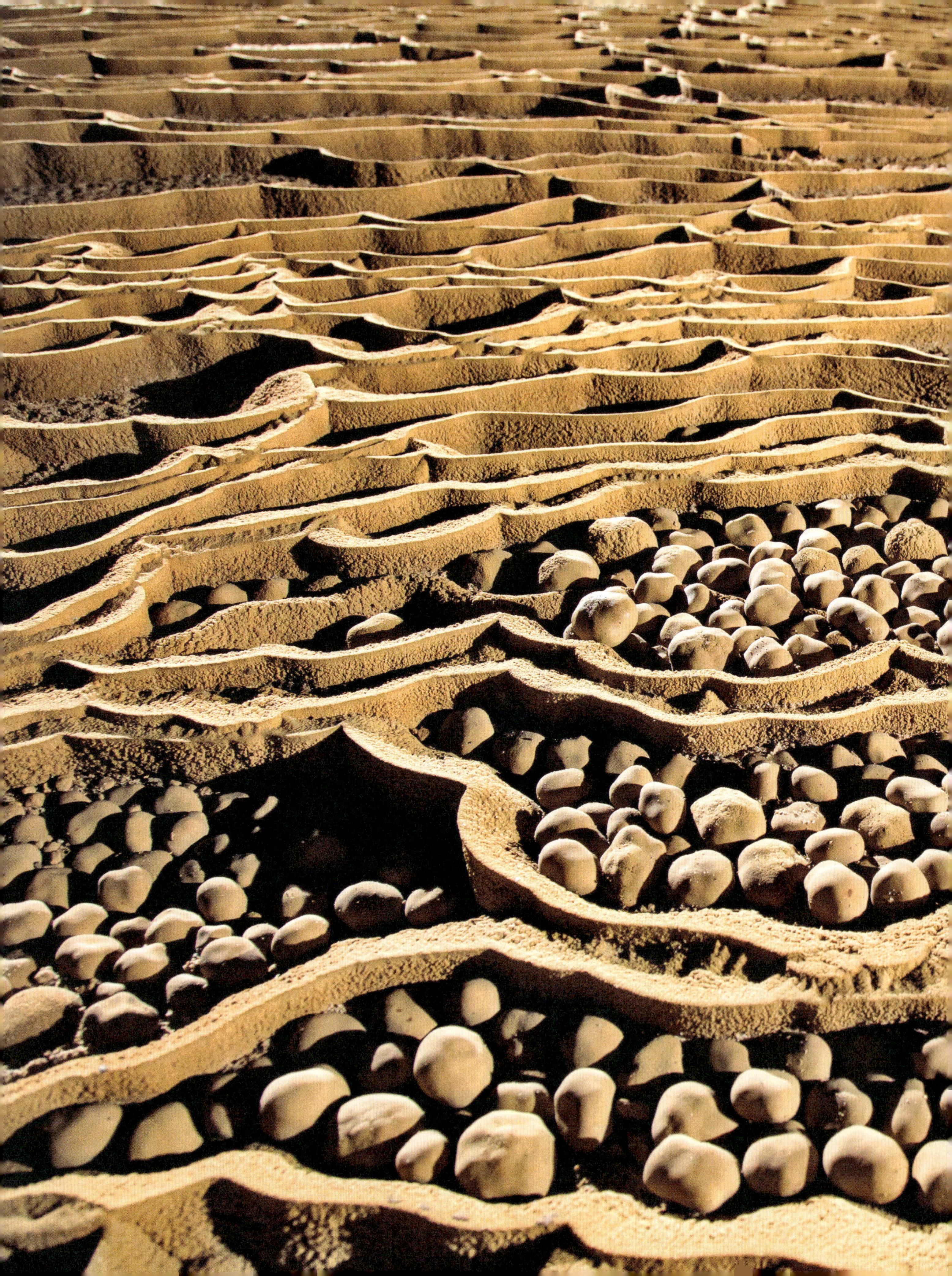

Some cave pearls are so shiny you can see your face in them, like a mirror.

Cave pearls

Despite sharing the same name, cave pearls are not real pearls at all. These "pearls" are round in shape, can be brown or white, and are sometimes shiny, like pearls. However, unlike real pearls, they do not come from the sea. Rather, they are found in caves made of limestone rock.

Cave pearls start out as specks of limestone rock, shell, or sand. These specks form what is called the nucleus of the pearl. When dripping water splashes onto the nucleus, it leaves traces of the mineral calcite. Over time, the layers of calcite build up, making the pearl bigger and bigger. Cave pearls grow on cave walls, ceilings, and on the cave floor, and are most often found in shallow pools of water.

Hang Son Doong cave in Phong Nha Ke Bang National Park, Vietnam, is home to a large number of rare cave pearls.

Ocean zones

The depth of the ocean varies – from sunlit shallows to deep, dark trenches. All kinds of wonderful sea creatures make their home at the different levels, or zones, of the ocean – from turtles, dolphins, and butterfly fish near the surface to seapigs and snailfish that live far, far down in the deepest parts of the ocean.

Sunlit zone

0–200 m (0–650 ft)
As the name suggests, this zone is bathed in sunlight, and this helps keep the temperature warm. Most ocean plants and animals live here.

Dolphin

Twilight zone

200–1,000 m (650–3,300 ft)
This zone is colder and darker, but there is still some light. At night, some animals swim up to the sunlit zone to feed.

Octopus

Midnight zone

1,000–4,000 m (3,300–13,000 ft)
No sunlight reaches the midnight zone, so it is completely dark and very cold. The only light comes from the particular animals that can produce their own light.

Anglerfish

Abyssal zone

4,000–6,000 m (13,000–20,000 ft)
Hardly anything at all lives in the freezing cold, inky-black waters or on the seafloor of this zone.

Seapig

Trench zone

6,000–11,000 m (13,000–36,000 ft)
Much deeper than most of the seafloor, trenches plunge down into the very depths of the ocean. Here, the pressure of the water is at its most intense.

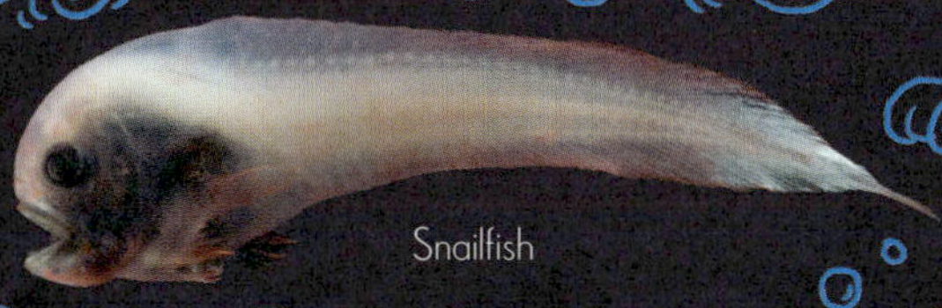
Snailfish

Smoking chimneys

The towers can reach up to about 55 m (180 ft) before they get too tall and fall over.

Deep down in the darkest reaches of the ocean floor there lurk strange-looking smoking chimneys. These are in fact hot springs, called hydrothermal vents or, simply, smokers.

Hydrothermal vents are found where new ocean crust is made. The chimneys are created when seawater seeps through cracks, or fissures, in the ocean crust and is heated by hot magma. The hot seawater, now rich in minerals, is pushed back to the surface through the vents. Seawater in hydrothermal vents can reach temperatures of more than 400°C (750°F). The water cools as it erupts into the cold ocean and the minerals build into mounds and towers.

Mineral-laden water spurts out of a hydrothermal vent on the Mid-Atlantic Ridge in the Atlantic Ocean.

Manganese nodules grow really slowly, by only a centimetre (half an inch) every million years.

Manganese nodules

Most nodules are between the size of a golf ball and a bowling ball.

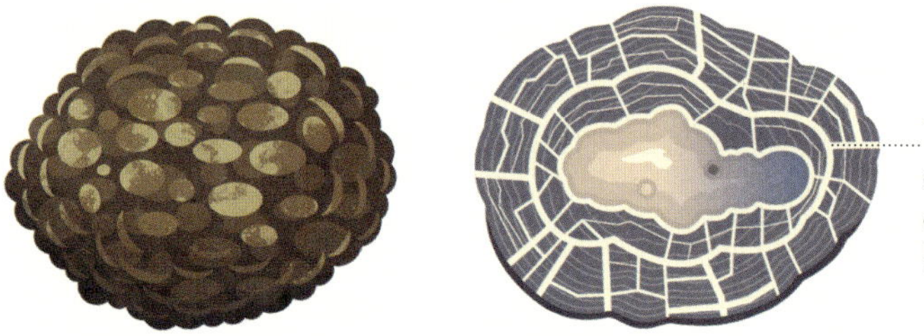

The nodule's layers are a bit like the rings on a tree trunk and show how it grows with time.

Large areas of the deep ocean remain shrouded in mystery. And there is a surprising find to be had on the floor of the ocean itself. Rather strangely, many areas of the seabed are covered with metallic lumps called manganese nodules. They take this name because manganese is the main metal they are made from. However, they also contain iron, nickel, cobalt, copper, and titanium.

Manganese nodules are found in all the world's oceans, but especially in a vast area of the Pacific Ocean off the coast of Mexico. How they form is a tale in itself – the metals dissolve in seawater, then slowly build up in layers around an object, such as a shell, bone, or a shark's tooth. In the future, these forgotten-about lumps may be collected from the bottom of the sea for the valuable metals they contain.

These manganese nodules are lying on the bed of the Atlantic Ocean.

It can take thousands of years for coccoliths to sink to the ocean floor.

This picture has been magnified many times to show the pretty patterns of the coccolith plates that encase the round-shaped coccospheres.

Ocean ooze

The ocean floor is covered in tiny particles of rocks and minerals called sediment. Some sediment grains are washed by rivers, ice, and wind into the sea from the land. Deep-ocean sediments, however, have a different story to tell. Called ooze, they are the remains of sea life mixed with chemicals in the water that sank down to the ocean floor.

Most ooze is calcareous – this means it is made up of chalky, calcium carbonate mud, produced by tiny single-celled, plant-like organisms, or phytoplankton, that float near the surface of the ocean. One major type of phytoplankton are called coccolithophores (ko-koh-lith-oh-fors). These are covered with round-shaped coverings, or coccospheres. Each coccosphere is surrounded by circular plates called coccoliths. There are millions, billions, and even trillions of coccolithophores in some areas of the ocean and their coccolith plates take many, many years to sink to the ocean floor. Here, they eventually make cream-coloured, calcareous ooze.

Tiny particles of sea life and other matter that gradually sink to the bottom of the ocean are called "marine snow".

Waves

Have you ever been to the seaside and watched the waves crashing onto the shore? Waves are powerful bursts of energy caused by the wind. They start out in the deep ocean. As wind begins to blow across the surface of the water, it makes the water rise and fall. First, ripples form, and then as the wind continues to blow, the ripples turn into waves – and the stronger the wind, the bigger the wave.

Finally, the wave finishes its journey and crashes, or breaks, onto the shore. It breaks because the top of the wave, called the crest, has literally toppled over! It has overtaken the water below, which was slowed down by the slope of the ground under the water. And as the wave breaks, the water sprays through the air, like white horses thundering in towards the shore.

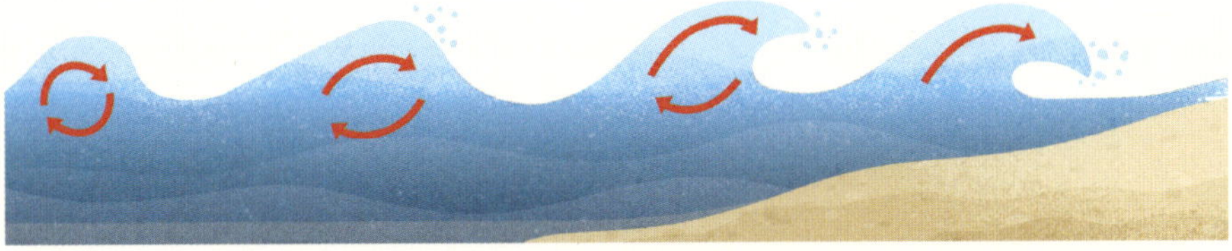

The water in each wave goes round in circles, passing energy to the water in front and moving the wave forwards until it crashes onto the shore.

Waves can reach heights of more than 20 m (60 ft).

This huge and powerful ocean wave is breaking during a stormy evening. Unusually big waves like this are called rogue or freak waves.

Whirlpool

Have you ever watched the water going down the plughole in the bath or sink? It swirls round and round. It is a little whirlpool. In nature, whirlpools can occur in fast-flowing rivers, or on a bigger scale out at sea. The largest ones of all are called maelstroms – fierce, violent swirls that can pull down entire ships.

Whirlpools happen when ocean water moving in one direction meets ocean water coming from another direction. The direction that the water moves in is called the current, and it keeps changing. When two fast-flowing currents meet like this, they try to get past each other without slowing down. Imagine you met someone coming towards you and neither of you wanted to slow down – you would have to move to go around each other. The currents do that, but then keep swirling round and round, making a whirlpool.

Giant whirlpools can be about 10 m (33 ft) across and 5 m (16 ft) deep.

Water moving in one direction meets water moving the opposite way.

If a whirlpool spirals downwards, it forms an empty space in the centre, called a vortex.

Coral reef

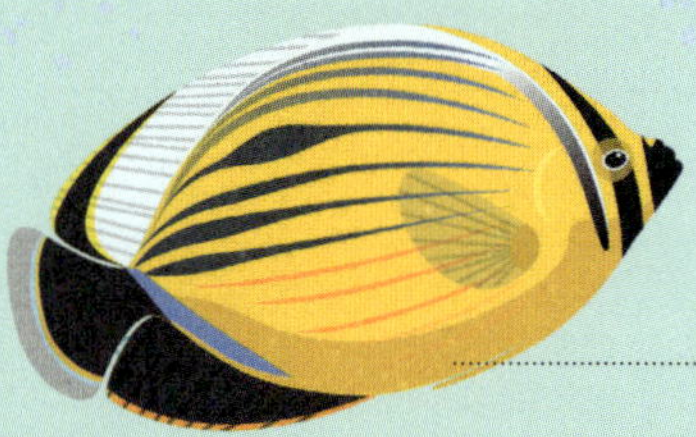

Stripy blacktail butterflyfish are native to the Red Sea, an inlet of the Indian Ocean.

Clownfish make their home in the warm tropical waters of coral reefs.

Some coral reefs have been growing for 30 million years.

Colourful coral reefs are teeming with life – fish and other sea creatures live here, and the reefs themselves are alive, too. A coral reef begins when millions of little tube-shaped animals called polyps attach themselves to submerged rocks by the seashore. A single polyp sprouts more polyps, and their hard, chalky skeletons link together to form a coral reef. This all takes a rather long time. Some corals only grow up to 2 cm (0.7 in) a year, so it can take the polyps 10,000 years to form a reef. This makes the coral reef the oldest ecosystem on Earth that is built by animals.

Here, fish swim among the coral in the Red Sea, in Egypt. The orange colours of the fish help them to hide from predators.

Coral atoll

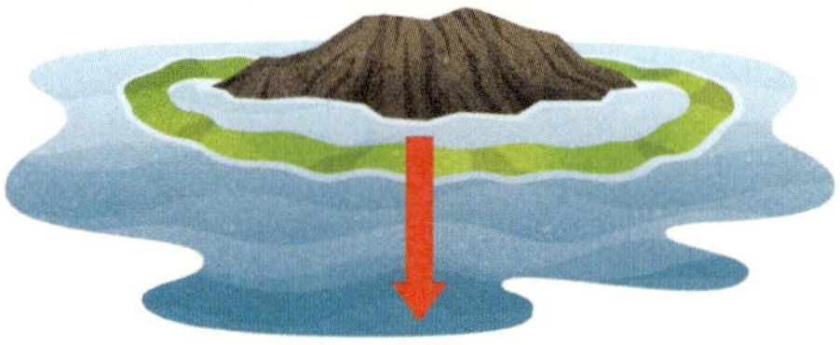

Some volcanic islands, surrounded by coral, sink beneath the ocean.

While the volcano disappears underwater, the coral reef remains at the surface.

The Pakin Atoll surrounds a beautiful blue lagoon in Micronesia in the Pacific Ocean.

An atoll is a ring-shaped reef, usually made of coral, that encircles a body of water, called a lagoon, sometimes with an island in the middle. Most atolls are in the Pacific Ocean, where it is warm enough for the corals to grow.

British scientist Charles Darwin was the first person to work out how atolls are made. He said that the atoll is what is left after a volcanic island has sunk below the sea. Before it sinks, coral grows in the warm, shallow water around its edge, as a fringing reef. As the volcano sinks and the sea level rises, the coral keeps growing – forming a barrier reef with a lagoon between the volcano and the coral. Eventually, the volcano disappears altogether so only the atoll is left.

Spanish explorer Isabel Barreto made one of the first recorded sightings of Pakin Atoll in 1595.

Kelp forests grow along a quarter of the world's coasts.

Kelp forest

Sea otters wrap themselves in kelp to anchor themselves to one place. The otters are important to the survival of kelp forests as they prey on sea urchins, which feed on kelp.

Kelp is a type of seaweed that grows in cool, shallow coastal waters around the world. Have a look for some when you next visit the seaside, as fronds can be washed onto the beach after storms. Where kelp grows really thick it resembles a forest, with the long fronds waving in the water like leaves moving in the wind. However, unlike trees, the kelp doesn't have roots. It is attached to the floor or a rock by a sticky holdfast that acts like an anchor as it grows up towards the light. Along the fronds there are floating air-filled sacs called pneumatocysts, which help to keep the fronds upright. If the little balloon-like sacs didn't do their job, the fronds would get tangled up along the seafloor.

The giant kelp has hundreds of kelp fronds and each frond can grow to be more than 30 m (100 ft) long.

Unlike other seaweed, sargassum is not attached to rocks, but forms a floating garden just beneath the waves.

Sargassum

A system of currents called a gyre encircle the Sargasso Sea.

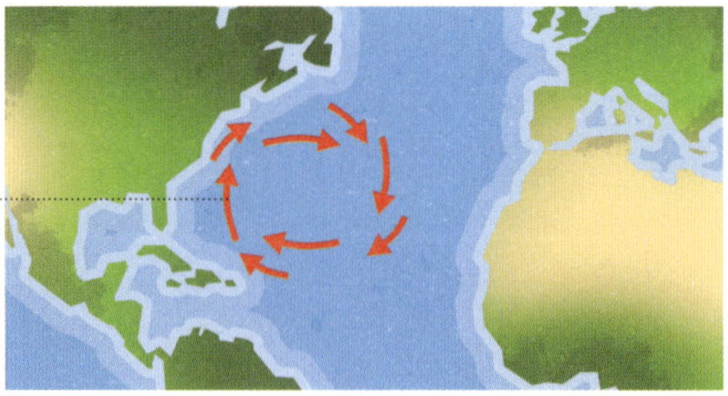

As well as floating in the Sargasso Sea, sargussum seaweed is found in shallow coastal waters and by coral reefs around the world. This sargassum is floating by the Raja Ampat Islands in Indonesia.

In the middle of the North Atlantic Ocean there is a large patch of calm, clear, blue water called the Sargasso Sea. These still waters form the perfect home for golden-brown seaweed called sargassum to grow.

The waters of the Sargasso Sea are calm because it lies at the centre of a system of circling ocean currents, called a gyre. The currents push the drifting seaweed into the calm waters, where it can thrive. The sargassum creates a haven for sea life, including eels, crab, fish, and baby turtles, who hide among the seaweed, safe from their enemies.

Red tide

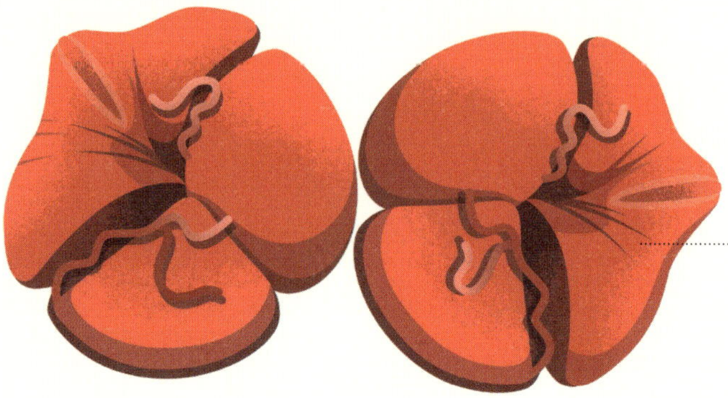

Tiny microalgae called *karenia brevis* cause red tide.

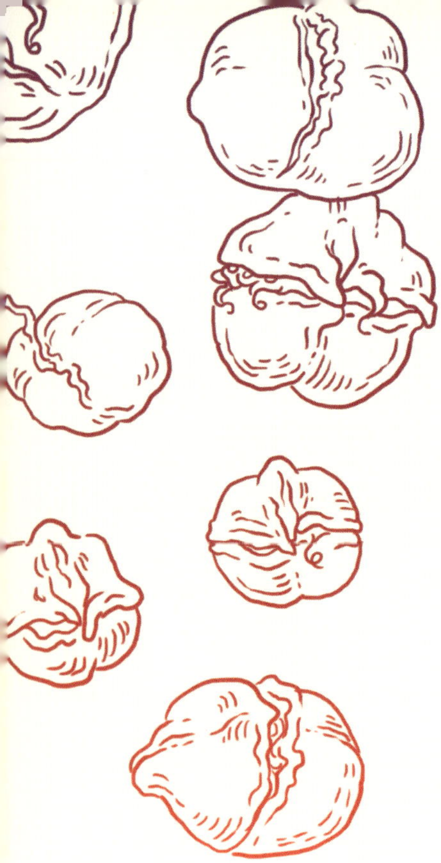

It may look striking, but a red tide spells danger. It is caused by harmful microalgae that turn water red. Microalgae are tiny, simple plant-like organisms that live in both sea- and freshwater. When there are lots of them and they flower like plants, they are called an algal bloom. Mostly, algal blooms are helpful, providing food for a variety of sea creatures, such as shrimp and jellyfish. However, if they grow out of control, they become dangerous. They can poison and kill shellfish and fish, and if you eat infected seafood, you can get very sick.

Red tides can be hard to predict, but fortunately don't usually last long – from a day to a few weeks. Because they are so dangerous, scientists even use special telescopes to search for them from space. They can then warn people where they are so they know not to fish or swim near them.

Red tides are not always red – the water can also appear brown, rusty orange, or even green.

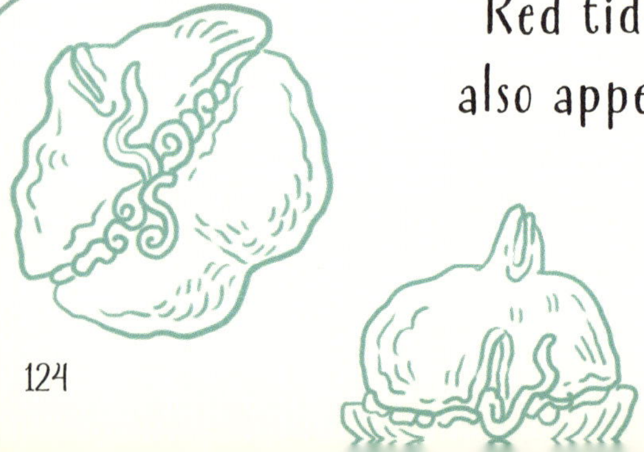

This algal bloom is by the Bountiful Islands, in the Gulf of Carpentaria in Queensland, Australia.

Polar regions

The Arctic and Antarctica are at opposite ends of the Earth. The Arctic is at the North Pole at the top, with Antarctica at the South Pole at the bottom. They are both vast, cold, empty regions covered in ice. However, while the Arctic is an ocean surrounded by land, Antarctica is a continent surrounded by ocean.

The Arctic

The North Pole is in the Arctic Ocean, which is covered by moving ice that melts in the summer and freezes in the winter. Unlike at the South Pole, there isn't a permanent marker at the North Pole because it is on moving ice above the sea. The North Pole is about 700 km (435 miles) away from Greenland.

Ice algae

Algae growing in the sea ice are called ice algae. The algae thrive in bubbles in the ice by trapping liquid water inside the bubbles. When the sea ice melts, the algae sink to the seabed and are fed on by animals and bacteria.

Mount Erebus

There are mountains, valleys, and even volcanoes on Antarctica, including Mount Erebus, the most southerly active volcano in the world. Here, you can see a plume of gases escaping from its crater, which holds a bubbling lava lake.

Weddell seals live and hunt on the Antarctic sea ice.

Antarctic mammals

Seals are the only mammals that live on land in Antarctica, and several species are found here. They live on ice or on the small islands that surround the continent.

Arctic mammals

Unlike in Antarctica, there are many mammals that make their home in the Arctic. These include polar bears, Arctic foxes, reindeer, and Arctic wolves. All these mammals have thick fur to protect them from the cold.

Polar bears play with their cubs on the Arctic ice.

Sea ice

Arctic sea ice can be around 1.8 m (6 ft) thick. However, in some areas, it compresses and piles up to form ice packs more than twice that thickness.

Sea ice is frozen seawater that floats on the ocean as thick sheets.

Midnight Sun

Both the Arctic and Antarctica have two long seasons. In the six months of winter, it is dark nearly all day and night. During the summer, it stays light. The Sun never sets, but stays low on the horizon. At midnight it is called the Midnight Sun.

Antarctica

Antarctica is the coldest, driest, and windiest of the continents, with wind speeds of up to 320 kph (200 mph). It is so dry, that it is classed as a desert! These conditions make it too cold to live there permanently. While people have lived in the Arctic region for thousands of years, in Antarctica every human is a visitor – a researcher, explorer, or a tourist.

Snow monsters

Maries' fir trees are native to Japan.

Like something out of a scary fairy tale, "snow monsters", or *juhyo*, appear every winter on the slopes of Mount Zao in Japan. However, there's no need to be frightened of these particular monsters – because they are actually fir trees covered in snow.

These conifers are evergreen, which means they don't lose their needles in winter. From late December until the middle of March, freezing cold winds blow from Arctic Siberia bringing lots of snow and ice. The snow can be several metres deep. And since the winds are so strong, the icicles that form are practically horizontal. The trees get covered again and again by layers of snow and ice, and that's how these tall, menacing snow monsters take shape.

Snow monsters can be about 30 m (100 ft) tall.

Snow and ice make the fir trees look like strange figures towering over the ground.

Glacier

Glaciers slide slowly downhill, reshaping the landscape as they go. If more snow and ice get added, the glacier is said to advance, or get bigger.

The front of a glacier is called the toe.

The Elephant Foot glacier is 5.4 km (3 miles) wide and can be seen from space!

Glaciers are frozen rivers of ice that flow slowly downhill. They can take thousands of years to form. Over time, snowfall piles up in layers, gradually pressing into the ice to eventually form a glacier. If the climate warms, glaciers melt. They tend to shrink from the bottom up – with the leading edge retreating back uphill – because higher temperatures are usually found at lower levels. If the climate stays cold, however, glaciers advance downhill until they reach the sea.

The extraordinary Elephant Foot Glacier in Greenland is called this because it is indeed the shape of an elephant's foot. This type of glacier is called a piedmont. It is formed when ice from a steep valley flows into a flat plain and spreads out into a fan shape.

The Elephant Foot Glacier
is in northeastern Greenland.

Sea ice

While icebergs break off from glaciers, sea ice is quite different, as it is made from seawater. In the winter, when it is freezing cold in Arctic and Antarctic waters, ice crystals grow on the surface of the salty sea. The water freezes into ice crystals, but the salt doesn't get used and so it sinks back into the ocean. Meanwhile, the freshwater ice crystals join together to make thin sheets of ice, like sheets of paper. Gradually, the ice sheets slide over each other and combine to make thicker rafts of sea ice, also called pack ice.

In winter, the rafts move, collide, and join together to cover vast areas of the sea, so that instead of looking blue, the surface of the sea looks white over many kilometres. The white surface reflects the heat of the Sun, like a mirror, into space. This is very useful as it helps keep ocean and air temperatures regular.

Icebergs break off from glaciers that have originated on land.

Sea ice comes from the ocean.

Sea ice provides a place to rest for seals, walruses, and other polar animals.

These crabeater seals are resting on the sea ice in Antarctica.

Stripy iceberg

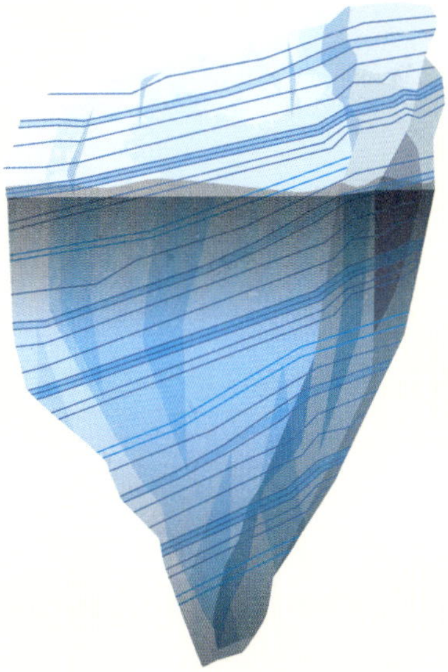

Only one-eighth of an iceberg can be seen above the surface – the rest is underwater.

This imposing, giant iceberg looms out of the freezing waters around 1,000 km (600 miles) north of Antarctica. It towers up to 9 m (30 ft) high and is around 45 m (150 ft) long. What is perhaps even more remarkable than its size, however, is the fact that it has blue stripes. These stripes are caused by water getting trapped in gaps in the ice and then freezing really fast – too fast to make bubbles. And it is the tiny air bubbles that spread out light and give most icebergs their usual white appearance.

Icebergs are large chunks of freshwater ice that have broken off a glacier and float freely in open water. Those icebergs with stripes are called striated icebergs, and the stripes are not always blue. If a glacier travels downhill over rocks, soil, or grit, it can pick up dirt at its base. And if an iceberg breaks off, the dirt can cause it to have brown, yellow, or black stripes. Microscopic algae that live in the sea can freeze as green stripes on some floating icebergs.

This striated iceberg was seen in the Southern Ocean, between South Africa and Antarctica.

Pure, blue glacier ice is hard, like rock, and does not melt easily.

Blue ice

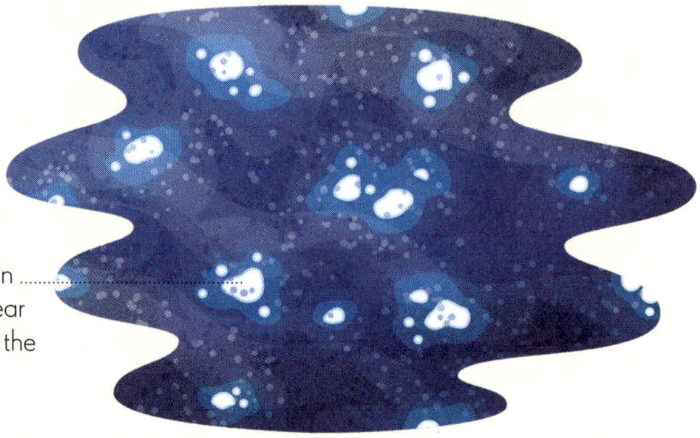

Tiny bubbles in blue ice appear white, due to the trapped air.

Out in freezing Antarctica, vast, blue-coloured glaciers loom up out of the sea. The ice looks blue for a reason. When layers of snow press down, they squash the snow beneath them into ice and squeeze out all the air bubbles. The more the white ice is squashed, the bluer it looks.

The ice is blue – and not red or green, for example – because of the way light travels. When all the colours of the rainbow are mixed together, such as in the air around us, they make white light. So when light passes through ice that has air bubbles in it, it looks white because it reflects all the colours. However, there is no air in thick, compacted ice. The result is that every colour of the rainbow gets absorbed, apart from blue – and the bigger the iceberg or glacier, the bluer it appears.

Here, a group of chinstrap penguins are resting on a blue iceberg in the Weddell Sea, Antarctica.

All year round, ice caves remain at temperatures below 0°C (32°F).

Ice cave

Lake Baikal in Siberia, Russia, is home to many ice caves. It is the deepest freshwater lake in the world and holds about 20 per cent of the world's freshwater.

Dazzling and shimmering in the winter sunshine, ice caves actually have ice in them all year round. Even in summer or when it is warmer outside, the water in the cave stays frozen. The cold air is trapped inside the cave and the warm air can't get in to melt the ice.

Ice caves are formed in several ways. Some, such as the Blue Ice Cave, are found in rocky caves that can form along the edge of frozen lakes. Other ice caves take shape in chambers that were once filled with water but are now frozen. Some ice caves are formed from inside a lava tube. This is a passageway that once had volcanic lava surging through it. Once the lava has left, it leaves behind a hollow passage. Then, if water flows into the passage, it freezes, forming an ice cave. Some such ice caves were once used by people to store food and keep it cold, before the electric fridge was invented.

The Blue Ice Cave is found in Lake Baikal, which is covered in thick sheets of ice between November and March.

If a waterfall freezes, stalactites and stalagmites may join together to create spectacular ice pillars.

Frozen waterfall

Rarely, waterfalls can freeze over, and when they do, they make beautiful intricate patterns of ice and snow. While it is easier for a small, slow-flowing stream to freeze, even fast-moving water can, too – especially in cold, windy places where the moving water becomes supercooled. This means the temperature of the moving water drops below the freezing point of 0°C (32°F) – and stays there.

When supercooled water freezes, it sets solid as a lump of tiny, needle-shaped crystals called frazil ice. Instead of the ice forming on the water's surface, the frazil ice sinks down and cools the water further so more ice crystals grow. Once a single layer of ice freezes, more layers build up to make a frozen waterfall.

This spectacular frozen waterfall is in Johnston Canyon in Banff National Park, Alberta, Canada.

The fastest gust of wind ever recorded was in Australia in 1996, at 407 kph (253 mph).

Air

Air is all around us, but usually we can't see it. We can, however, feel the air blowing on a windy day, and can often see clouds. When it rains, we know that the water that was held invisible in the air is now falling and making us wet. The air that we breathe is just one of the many layers that make up the atmosphere. This is the layer closest to the surface of our planet. The one in which we live, and here there is plenty of oxygen for us to breathe. If you climb up the highest mountains, where the air holds less oxygen, we say the air is "thin". Climbers may need to take oxygen with them to breathe.

Most weather conditions – such as rain, hail, and snow – happen in this lowest layer. On a sunny day, the sky is blue, and when there is rain, a colourful rainbow may appear. When it is stormy, you might see lightning and hear the clap of thunder as electricity surges through the air. And in certain places, you might gaze at an aurora display, with moving curtains of green, blue, red, and purple.

Clockwise from top: aurora borealis in Kirkjufell mountains, Iceland; a flag tree misshapen by the wind, Tierra Del Fuego, Argentina; an ice halo; and a landspout tornado, Kansas, USA.

Earth's atmosphere

Earth is protected by a blanket of gases called the atmosphere. It keeps the planet's temperature steady, blocking out the Sun's harmful rays. The atmosphere is made up of five layers. The troposphere is the closest to us and gives us the air that we breathe.

The Hubble Space Telescope orbits the Earth in the exosphere.

The Kármán line is the rough boundary line between Earth's atmosphere and the beginning of space.

The International Space Station orbits within the thermosphere.

Most **meteor** burn up on en the mesospher

Exosphere

This is the final layer of atmosphere before reaching airless outer space. There is no weather in the exosphere. This is where most of Earth's satellites orbit. It reaches about halfway to the Moon.

700–10,000 km (440–6,200 miles) above the Earth's surface.

Thermosphere

The lowest part contains the ionosphere, where Earth's atmosphere meets space. Temperatures increase with altitude, and sometimes the aurora borealis and aurora australis appear.

80–700 km (50–440 miles) above the Earth's surface.

Mesosphere

The mesosphere gets colder the higher up you go. The top of the mesosphere is the coldest part of the atmosphere, with an average temperature of about -85°C (-120°F).

50–80 km (31–50 miles) above the Earth's surface.

The stratosphere is the highest layer that **jet planes** can fly in.

Earth's weather happens in the troposphere. It is the only layer where we can breathe naturally. **Hot-air balloons** can fly at this level.

Stratosphere

The Earth's ozone layer, protecting us from the Sun's harmful ultraviolet radiation, is in the stratosphere. Because of the ultraviolet rays, the higher up you go, the warmer temperatures become.

12–50 km (7.5–31 miles) above the Earth's surface.

Troposphere

The higher up you go in the troposphere, the colder it gets. This is because most of the heat is being generated from the Earth's surface, which has been heated by the Sun.

Up to about 12 km (7.5 miles) above the Earth's surface.

Early atmosphere

Planet Earth was formed about 4.5 billion years ago. During its first 500 million years, huge volcanic eruptions spewed out water vapour and other gases. It was this activity that formed the oceans and the atmosphere.

Volcanoes release large amounts of carbon dioxide, with little or no oxygen. Water vapour is also produced.

The water vapour released from volcanoes condenses as the Earth cools down, eventually forming the oceans.

Carbon dioxide dissolves into the ocean. Later, plants and tiny organisms evolve, absorbing CO_2 and releasing oxygen.

Auroras

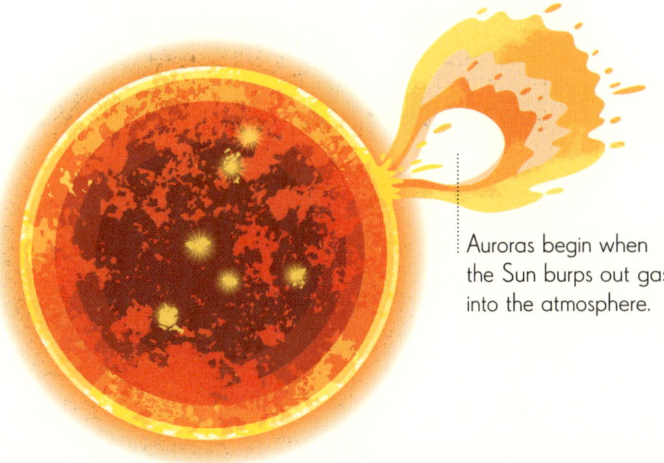

Auroras begin when the Sun burps out gas into the atmosphere.

Astronauts in space can see the auroras when orbiting Earth.

At night, weird and wonderful shapes and curtains of colour can be seen moving in the sky. These beautiful light shows last about 30 minutes at a time. They are called auroras, or polar lights, because you can only see them near the poles. At the North Pole, they are called the northern lights, or aurora borealis, while the southern lights at the South Pole are known as aurora australis.

Auroras are made by the Sun when it sends out energy in the form of electrified gas during a solar storm. If the energy is attracted towards the North and South magnetic poles of the Earth and the gas reaches our atmosphere, it creates colourful patterns in the sky. The red and green colours are made by oxygen gas, while purple and blue colours are created by nitrogen gas.

Aurora borealis lights up the sky over a frozen lake in Lofoten, Norway.

These trees on Slope Point in New Zealand cannot grow straight because the wind always blows from the same direction.

Wind

Warm air rises and cool air falls below it, creating wind.

The windiest place on Earth is Antarctica, where wind speeds reach around 320 kph (200 mph).

Air certainly doesn't like to stay still, and wind is moving air. Changes in the temperature of land, sea, and air combine to cause wind. When air warms up, it rises, and when it cools down, it sinks and moves in underneath the warmer air above it. If you're outside, you might feel wind as a gentle breeze on your face, or you might be tempted to fly a kite in stronger, gustier wind.

Winds move the clouds and bring rain and snow. Powerful winds can cause storms or even tornadoes and hurricanes. In some places, such as at Slope Point, the southernmost tip of New Zealand, the wind is so strong and so consistent that it can change the shape of the trees, forcing them to grow over to one side.

Clouds form when water vapour rising high into the sky cools. Cold air cannot hold as much moisture as warm air, so the water vapour condenses to form clouds.

Clouds

Clouds come in all shapes and sizes, and usually form in the lowest layer of Earth's atmosphere, called the troposphere. They look different depending on their height above the ground and how the wind is blowing. High-level clouds include noctilucent, which appear after sunset on warm summer evenings, and pink-coloured nacreous, which are only seen at the polar regions. Middle-level clouds include the drooping and bulbous-looking mammatus, which are often a sign of thundery weather. Also to be found at this level are disc-shaped lenticular clouds, which stack up like pancakes in the sky and are often found near mountainous areas. At lower levels in the sky, rippling, wave-like asperitas clouds can be found, as well as the more common white, puffy stratocumulus.

Lenticular clouds have been mistaken for flying saucers!

From left to right, top to bottom: glowing noctilucent clouds; colourful nacreous clouds; rounded mammatus clouds; pancake-shaped lenticular clouds; rippling asperitas clouds; and puffy stratocumulus clouds.

Storm cloud

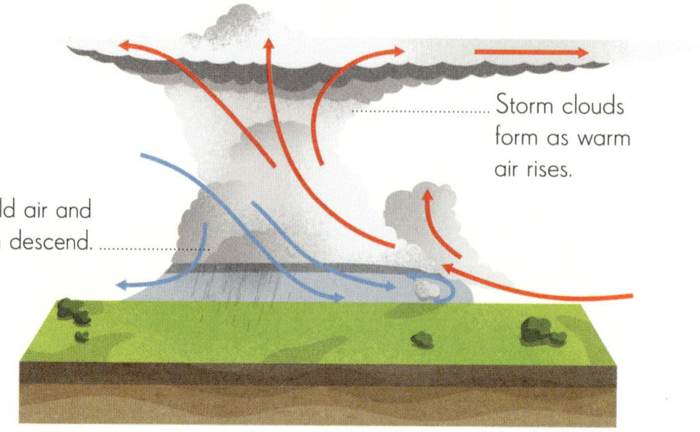

Mammatus clouds can be seen most clearly when lit up by the Sun. The bulbous shapes hang down on average about 0.5 km (0.3 miles) at the bottom of the cloud.

The cumulonimbus is also known as the King of Clouds. These clouds look like huge towers reaching high up into the sky. They are thunderclouds, and are the only type of cloud that can make rain, hail, thunder, and lightning.

Usually, the base of a cumulonimbus cloud is flat, but sometimes the base sprouts what look like hanging balloons filled with water. These heavy, rounded pouches are called mammatus clouds. And once they get too heavy and full of water, the rains fall and a storm breaks out.

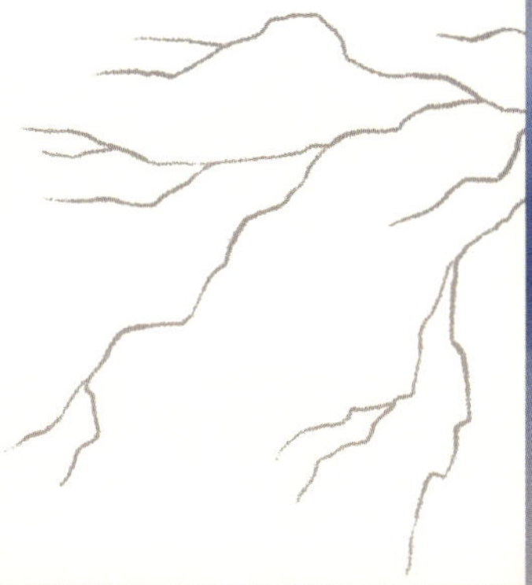

The hanging pouch of a mammatus cloud can be up to 3 km (2 miles) across.

Rain

Most of Earth's surface is covered in water – salt water that we cannot drink. So freshwater from rain is essential for life on Earth. It fills rivers and lakes, and keep plants and animals alive.

In warmer climates, rain forms when tiny droplets of water collect in clouds. Whenever the droplets get big enough, they fall to the ground as raindrops. Smaller droplets fall more slowly than big ones. If they are particularly small – less than 0.5 mm (0.02 in) – they form drizzle. Soft drizzle falls so slowly that it usually evaporates before it reaches the ground. In colder climates, ice crystals in clouds may join together to form snowflakes – and these can melt and fall as rain, too. Lack of rain can cause droughts, but too much rain can lead to flooding, especially in flat, low-lying areas.

A raindrop takes about two minutes to fall to the ground.

In this picture, heavy rain falls from a mushroom-shaped rain cloud that has formed over the North Sea near the island of Lindisfarne, England.

The swirling, rising warm air in a tornado meets cool, descending air.

A tornado can reach a height of 1.6 km (1 mile).

Tornado

Also called whirlwinds or twisters, tornadoes are powerful spinning columns of wind that can leave a trail of destruction. Strong tornadoes can pick up dust and rubbish, and trees and cars, and can even rip roofs off houses. These spiralling winds can reach speeds of up to 500 kph (300 mph), stretch more than 3 km (2 miles), and travel for more than 100 km (60 miles) along the ground.

Tornadoes usually form during storms. Inside thunderclouds, warm, moist air rises up and meets cool air, which falls and drops rain or hail. The warm and cool moving air currents can spin round and round in a circle. If the spinning air currents climb upwards and then drop downwards to connect the cloud to the ground, they create a funnel-shaped tornado.

Tornadoes often form on wide, open expanses of flat land, such as here in Colorado, USA.

The foggiest place in the world is Grand Banks, in Canada – it is foggy there on more than 200 days a year.

Fog

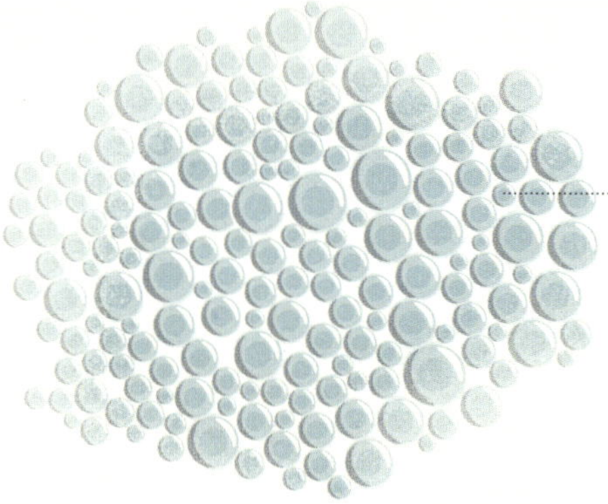

Fog forms from lots of tiny water droplets.

Did you know that if you're walking through fog, you are walking through a cloud? Land fog is quite simply a cloud that is touching the ground. Air usually holds some water vapour, but it is a gas, and you cannot see it. Humid air holds so much water vapour that it feels damp. In the evening, if this warm, humid air gets cooled by the cold ground, the vapour turns into water droplets. And if there are enough of these tiny water droplets, then you can see them – as fog.

Land fog occurs in the morning, mainly in sheltered valleys and low-lying fields. A foggy morning soon disappears – the fog is warmed by the Sun, blown away by wind, or washed away by rain.

Fog fills the valleys below the Te Mata Peak in Hawkes Bay, New Zealand.

Hailstone

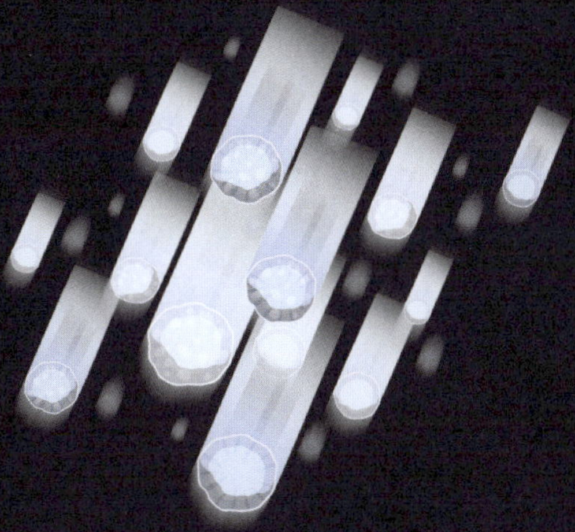

Made of solid ice, hailstones form when water freezes near the top of thunderclouds. Water drops are taken up by winds called updrafts and taken down in downdrafts – a process that happens again and again. Each time the water drops go up and down in the cloud, another layer of ice is added, and the hailstones gradually grow. The layers can be cloudy or clear. If it freezes quickly, the new icy layer is cloudy because the bubbles haven't had time to form. If it freezes more slowly, the layer of ice is mostly clear.

Hailstones fall from the sky when they are too heavy for the updrafts to hold them up. If they fall quickly, they don't have time to melt and they land as hailstones. Most hailstones are about the size of a pea and fall at about 16 kph (10 mph), but others can be much larger and fall a lot faster.

A hailstone can reach the size of a grapefruit and fall at speeds of 160 kph (100 mph).

This close-up of a hailstone shows the cloudy centre surrounded by a layer of clear, bubbly ice.

Ice storm

Ice is 10 times heavier than wet snow.

Unlike other storms, ice storms are strangely quiet, but they can still be deadly. Ice storms are also called "glaze events", because very cold rain gently covers everything in a silvery-white coating, or glaze. The rain isn't frozen, but rather supercooled, and when it lands on anything even colder, like a tree or a metal powerline, it freezes as a layer of ice.

As more layers build up, the ice gets so heavy it can cause a lot of damage. Trees and tree branches that start by looking very pretty snap off. Powerlines can break, and people are left without heat or light. One of the worst ice storms was in December 1964 in New York City, USA, when the ice became nearly 4 cm (1.5 in) thick.

This is a frozen wildflower after an ice storm.

Snowflakes

Snowflakes appear white as they float to the ground, but they are actually colourless.

Smaller snowflakes with six simpler arms are formed from cold clouds.

Large snowflakes with six decorative arms are formed from freezing clouds.

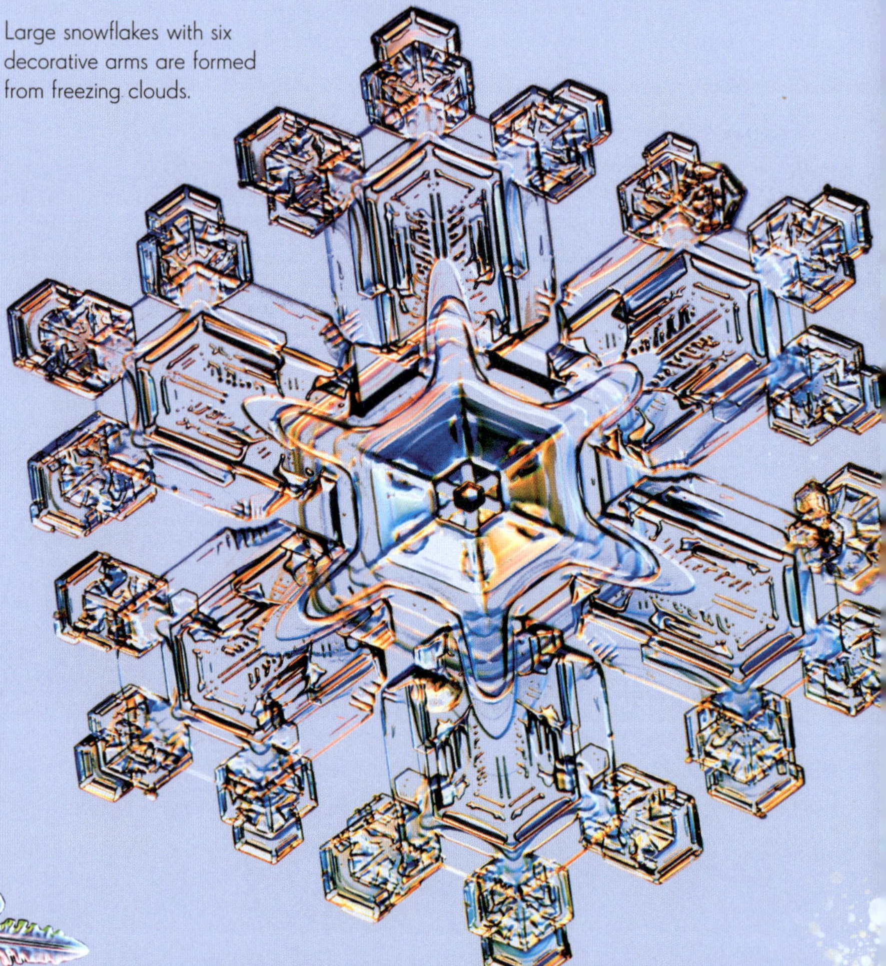

No two snowflakes are ever the same.

If it is cold enough, droplets of water in the clouds high above your head freeze to form ice crystals. These ice crystals stick together, getting bigger and bigger until they are so heavy they fall from the clouds as snowflakes.

To the naked eye, snowflakes look like fluffy white crumbs but if you look at snowflakes under a microscope, you will see that each one has its own individual pattern. Every snowflake starts as a little hexagon with six sides and each one grows six arms, but they each take a different path to the ground, passing through different temperatures and amounts of moisture in the air. It is this very journey that determines the eventual shape and design of a snowflake.

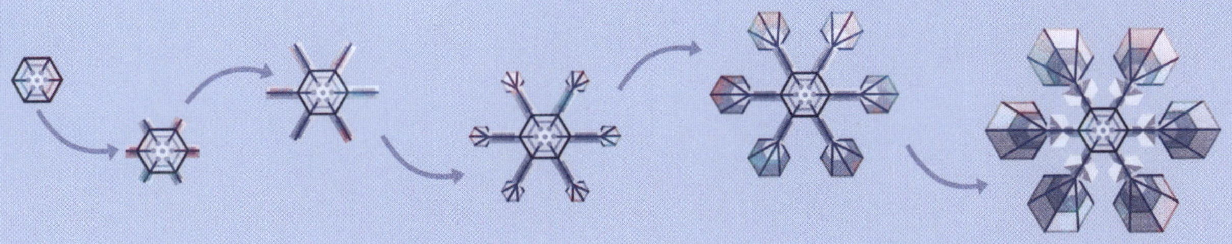

It was the British scientist Isaac Newton who first described how a rainbow works.

Rainbow

The curved shape that makes the bow is called an arc.

Have you ever seen a rainbow in the sky and wondered why it's there? Well, you may have noticed rain clouds and sunshine at the same time, too. This is because to make a rainbow, light from the Sun needs to shine through water droplets, such as those in rain clouds, waterfalls, or sea spray.

Sunlight is made up of different wavelengths of light. Each wavelength has a colour, but when mixed up, the colours produce white sunlight. When sunlight passes through raindrops, it bends, as it would if it passes through glass, and separates out the seven different colours of a rainbow. The colours, from the outside of the arc to the inside, are always: red, orange, yellow, green, blue, indigo, and violet.

When you see a rainbow, the Sun will always be behind you and the rain in front of you. This stunning rainbow is looming up out of the southern Atlantic Ocean, with the mountains of South Georgia island in the distance.

Bows and halos

All bows would actually make full circles, but you usually only see an arc or semi-circle because the rest is cut off by the horizon.

Did you know that as well as rainbows there are other types of "bows" that light up the sky? Fogbows occur where the light is spread by tiny water droplets in fog. They usually appear white or with very faint colours in the sky. This is because, unlike rainbows, the water droplets in fog are too small to bend sunlight enough for the colours to separate properly. A halo, or icebow, is produced when sunlight is reflected by ice crystals in the sky to make a white or colourful bow or halo circle. Moonbows are a little different – they are made by light from the Moon shining on water droplets, and they only occur at night.

The moonbow was first observed by the Greek philosopher Aristotle in 350 BCE.

From top to bottom: a fogbow shines over sea ice, in Svalbard, Norway; a halo forms around the Sun in winter in Saxony, Germany; and a double moonbow arcs around the Moon at night.

Everlasting storm

The electrical energy from Catatumbo lightning is strong enough to light 100 million lightbulbs.

As the Sun sets on Lake Maracaibo in Venezuela, a sudden flash of light illuminates the sky and turns night into day – again and again and again. This is Catatumbo lightning. "Catatumbo" means "house of thunder" in the language of the Bari people, who live near the lake. The lightning strikes Lake Maracaibo at the mouth of the Catatumbo River around 28 times a minute for up to 9 hours.

It is the lake's unique location that causes this strange event to take place. Lake Maracaibo is surrounded by a wall of mountains, leaving only a narrow channel open to the Caribbean Sea. All night long, strong winds whip the warm air from the sea and the lake upwards so that they collide with the colder air in the sky, producing the lightning. As the rising Sun signals the start of a new day, all is still and silent again – but only until the next lightning storm.

Catatumbo lightning is also known as the Maracaibo beacon, as sailors have used the light to guide them.

A polygon-shaped mud block usually has five or six sides.

The oldest mudcracks on Earth are more than 1 billion years old.

Mudcracks

When it hasn't rained for a long, long time it causes a drought. There is very little water in lakes, rivers, and streams and they might even dry out completely. In some places, there isn't enough fresh water to drink. People save water in specially built artificial lakes called reservoirs, and if even these dry out, there isn't enough water for people to use in their homes. Plants dry out and may die.

In really hot, dry weather, wet ground dries and cracks and makes mudcracks. These cracks make shapes called polygons that form amazing patterns in the mud. The mudcracks dry out from the surface downwards, so the crack is wider at the top and thins at the bottom. Geologists use them to work out the age of rocks. Anything above the top of the mudcracks is younger and anything below is older.

This picture shows the dried and cracked bed of Lake Burdur in Turkey.

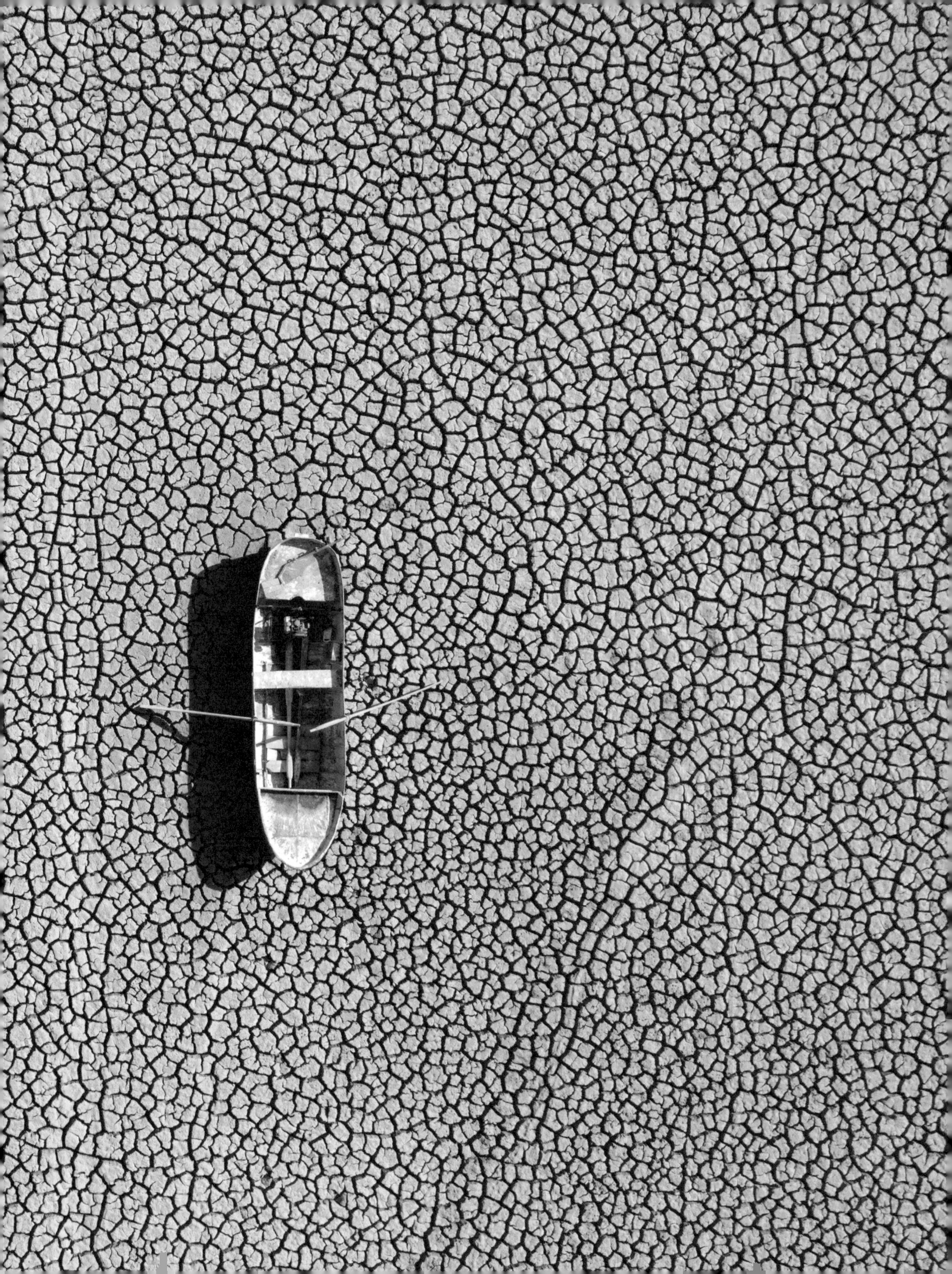

Landscapes

If you were to travel from the top of the world to the bottom, you would encounter many different landscapes and climates. You might start at the Arctic region of the North Pole, where it is freezing cold. As you travel towards the equator, the weather gets hotter and the landscape changes. There, you will see grasslands, low shrubs, trees, and temperate and tropical forests. There may be swamps, wetlands, flooded land, and even land reclaimed from the sea.

It isn't only the vegetation that changes – you will see mountains, deserts, hills, and valleys along the way. Towards the bottom of the world, it will get colder and the landscape will change again until you reach the frozen South Pole. The weather alters landscapes: weathering and erosion wear away mountains, break down rocks, and move rock fragments downhill and along valleys towards the sea.

Even desert landscapes can vary greatly, from the sand dunes of the Sahara, North Africa, to the cactus trees of the Mojave, USA.

Top to bottom: autumn trees; a forest in Acatenango, Guatemala; Erg Chebbi sand dunes, Sahara Desert, Morocco; and camels in the Gobi Desert, Mongolia.

More than half the world's plant and animal species are found in rainforests.

Mountain

Mountains are cold and windy, and often steep and rocky. The higher up the mountain, the colder and windier it is.

Polar

The Arctic and Antarctic polar regions are the coldest areas on Earth and are usually covered in ice. Few plants grow here.

Biomes

The areas of the Earth that share similar climate and vegetation, and where particular plants and animals live, are called biomes, or habitats. Earth can be divided into 10 biomes, ranging from dry deserts to green and fertile rainforests.

- Mountain
- Polar
- Tundra
- Taiga
- Desert
- Tropical rainforest
- Tropical grasslands
- Mediterranean
- Temperate grassland
- Temperate forest

Temperate forest

Temperate forests have four seasons and a mild climate. Here grow deciduous trees, such as oak, which shed their leaves in winter.

Temperate grassland

Called pampas in South America, prairie in North America, and steppe in Asia, these areas have grasses and shrubs.

Tundra

For most of the year, tundra ound freezes solid as permafrost. ere, hardy shrubs, grasses, and mosses grow.

Taiga

Cold taiga (boreal) forests have long winters and short summers. The trees are called conifers and have needles instead of leaves.

Desert

Few plants and animals live in dry desert lands. Some are hot and sunny, others are cold polar deserts.

Tropical rainforest

Tropical rainforests are warm and wet. The trees grow easily, as it rains almost every day.

Mediterranean

Forests and scrubland make up much of the plant life of this coastal biome with its hot, dry summers and warm, rainy winters.

Tropical grasslands

Also called savanna or plains, dry glasslands are covered in short and tall grasses with little tree coverage.

Hot desert

An oasis is a source of life in a hot, dry desert. Plants grow and animals can drink from the freshwater.

The Sahara Desert covers nearly one-third of Africa.

As you can tell from their name, hot deserts are not only dry, they are very, very hot, with scorching temperatures reaching more than 40°C (100°F) in the day. At night, however, they turn bitterly cold – with temperatures falling below freezing.

Most hot deserts are near the equator, which is an imaginary line around the middle of the Earth. The Sahara is the largest hot desert of them all – it extends right across North Africa. The continent is also home to one of the smallest hot deserts – the Namib. You might think that hot deserts only have sand and sand dunes, but sometimes there are mountains and valleys, and the ground is covered in large boulders or small rocks. And as you journey across barren sand and rock, you may come across the welcome sight of a green and fertile oasis.

This dromedary camel is standing in the Erg Chebbi dunes of the Sahara Desert in North Africa. The dunes are created by the wind blowing sand grains about and depositing them in heaps.

Cold desert

A small tree called the saxaul lives in the Gobi Desert – its trunk and branches are often bent and shaped by the wind.

Perhaps surprisingly, not all deserts are hot. In fact, the largest desert in the world is a cold desert – Antarctica – and this doesn't even have any sand. A desert is any place that has less than 25 cm (10 in) of rainfall a year and this includes the North Pole in the Arctic and the South Pole in Antarctica.

Another massive cold desert is the Gobi in Central Asia. This is a bit different to the Arctic and Antarctic deserts as it does actually have some sand – though not very much because it's mostly rocky. One remarkable part of the Gobi, however, is called Khongorn Els, which has snow-covered sand dunes that extend for around 100 km (62 miles) and can be up to 300 m (980 ft) high.

Khongorn Els is known as "the singing sands" because of the sound of the wind blowing across the dunes.

The Bactrian camel is one of the very few animals that can survive in the harsh climate of the Gobi Desert.

In the White Desert in Farafra, Egypt, the mushroom-shaped pedestal rocks are made of white quartz sandstone or white limestone.

The largest mushroom rock is in Kansas, USA – it is about 8 m (27 ft) wide.

Mushroom rock

Desert winds erode rocks into many different shapes.

It might seem strange to think of it, but millions of years ago the White Desert of Egypt was a seabed. When the sea eventually dried up, the bodies of millions of sea creatures calcified, which means they hardened and changed into calcium carbonate. This led to the creation of a vast plain of chalky limestone.

Desert winds carry lots of sand. Over time, the constant battering of the wind scoured the rocks, resulting in strange rock shapes, such as mushroom pedestals. They are this shape because the soft rocks near the bottom get eroded more easily than the harder rocks at the top.

Sandy beaches often form in sheltered bays, with gentler waves. Here, the sand gradually builds up and is not washed away.

Garnet sand

Sand

When we think of sand, we probably imagine golden "sandy" coloured beaches or deserts. This type of sand is made from rounded grains of quartz. However, sand can come in all kinds of shades, depending on the type of rock and the colour of the minerals contained in the rock. For example, black volcanic basalt rock makes black sand, and if it contains the mineral olivine, it makes the grains green. In parts of India and Spain, red sandy beaches can be found that are made from red garnets formed in metamorphic rock. Many beautiful white sandy beaches are made of crushed coral and shells, while the white beaches found in Hawaii are made from the poop of parrotfish.

Mineral sand

Shell sand

Volcanic sand

Desert sand

Olivine sand

Grains of rock with a width of
0.06–2 mm (0.002–0.08 in)
qualify as sand.

Karst

As rainwater seeps through the soft limestone, it gradually wears away the rock.

As more water collects, the cracks get wider, and rivers and caves form underground.

The cave roofs collapse, and rising sea levels erode the landscape, leaving towers.

There is a particularly unusual landscape that is made up of limestone hills, valleys, and flat plains. It gets its name, karst, from the flat Karst Plateau in Europe, which covers parts of Slovenia and Italy. However, the largest and most striking examples of karst lie in Southeast Asia and southern China, where vast areas of spiky limestone hills are surrounded by rice fields or water.

Karst owes its peculiar landscape to the fact that limestone is a soft rock and is easily shaped by the weather to form amazing rock formations. Rainwater soon seeps through any cracks in the soft rock and gradually wears it away, causing holes to form at the surface called sink holes. The water then travels deeper still and forms underground rivers and caves. Sometimes, people swim in the flooded sink holes, cave pools, and underground streams.

The karst landscape of southern China was formed more than 250 million years ago.

Karst hills loom up in the Guangxi region of southern China.

Savanna

There are some parts of the world that are too hot and dry for fertile green forests to grow, and yet get enough rainfall to stop them becoming deserts. These are tropical grasslands, called savannas. Here, most of the plants are grasses, with a few shrubs and trees that dot the landscape. The weather is mainly warm and dry, though there is a wet season. There are savannas in tropical areas throughout the world, but most are in Africa.

The African savanna supports herds of animals, such as giraffes, zebras, elephants, and gazelles. There is even a little antelope called a dik-dik, whose name comes from the "dik-dik" sound that the female makes.

The dik-dik lives in the grasslands of eastern and southern Africa.

Almost half of the continent of Africa is covered in savanna grasslands.

Here, zebras graze on African savanna plains surrounded by tall acacia trees.

The word "temperate" means "not extreme".

Temperate forest

Snow-covered in winter, with blossom in spring and green leaves in summer that turn gold in the autumn, temperate forests are shaped by the seasons. The trees are deciduous, which means they shed their leaves every year. These forests are neither too hot nor too cold. This is because of where they sit on Earth, lying roughly in two middle bands between the poles and the equator. Because of warm summers and cool winters, with lots of rain, a wide variety of plants can flourish here.

Below the trees – which include oak, ash, and beech – ferns and mosses grow, while in the spring, the ground may be carpeted with bluebells. In the autumn, people like to go on "fungus forays", looking for mushrooms on the forest floor.

These deciduous trees are showing their autumn colours of reds, browns, and oranges in the White Mountains of New Hampshire, USA.

The rainbow eucalyptus tree can grow about 1 m (3 ft) each year.

Rainbow eucalyptus

Rainbow eucalyptus trees grow in the tropical rainforests of Indonesia, Papua New Guinea, and the Philippines.

The beautiful rainbow eucalyptus tree is the only eucalyptus found in tropical rainforests. This fast-growing tree can reach heights of up to 75 m (246 ft) – as high as a 20-storey building.

The rainbow eucalyptus was first described and named in Indonesia in 1850. Because of its extraordinary bark, it was given the name *Eucalyptus deglupta* – the Latin word *deglupta* means "peeled off". On the outside, the bark is orange. However, as the tree grows, the bark peels off in strips and rainbow colours of red, orange, yellow, green, blue, and purple are revealed.

The inner layer of the rainbow eucalyptus is green, and the other colours appear according to how long each part of the bark has been exposed to the air.

Cloud forest

Discovered in 2013, the little olinguito makes its home in the cloud forests of Colombia and Ecuador.

While most tropical rainforests grow in low places, cloud forests are found high up in the mountains and are constantly shrouded in clouds. This creates a special damp environment that allows unique species of plants and animals to live and thrive.

The trees of cloud forests take in water not just from their roots but through their leaves, too. There is so much water in the clouds that water droplets land on the leaves and make them wet. This is called fog drip. Water that isn't absorbed by the leaves at the top of the trees drips down to be taken in by other leaves, while the rest waters plants lower down on the forest floor.

Cloud forests make up just one per cent of Earth's forests.

This is a view of a cloud forest in the Chocó region of northwest Ecuador.

Taiga

The tough little cloudberry plant lives in taiga forests across the world.

Meaning "land of the little sticks" in Russian, taiga forests are cold and lonely places. They are also called boreal forests, named after Boreas, the Greek god of the cold north wind.

These regions are found only in the northern half of Earth – just south of the icy Arctic region – in northern North America, Scandinavia, and Russia. In the long winters that last for more than half the year, temperatures are usually below freezing and it snows, heavily. The short summers are warm and bring rain. The trees that grow here are conifers – spruce, fir, and pine. They have tough, needle-shaped leaves that can survive the freezing temperatures.

About one-third of all the forests on Earth are taiga.

This snow-covered taiga forest is in Quebec, Canada.

Forest trees

While forest trees vary in size and shape, they need to grow tall because they're competing with each other for light. The prize for the largest tree in the world goes to a giant sequoia from California, USA, called General Sherman, with a trunk that is around 10 m (33 ft) wide. But the closely related redwood is the tallest, at about 116 m (380 ft).

You can tell what species a tree is by its shape, its leaves, and by the colour, patterns, and feel of the bark. The bark plays an important role in protecting the tree from insects and fungi, and it stops the tree from drying out. Young trees have smooth barks, and as the tree ages, the bark becomes cracked and peels, resulting in a wonderful range of textures and colours.

The world's oldest known tree is a bristlecone pine called Methuselah. It grows in the White Mountains of California and is more than 4,850 years old.

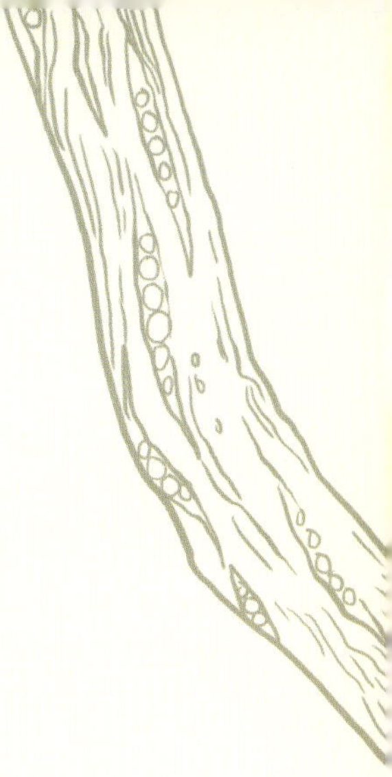

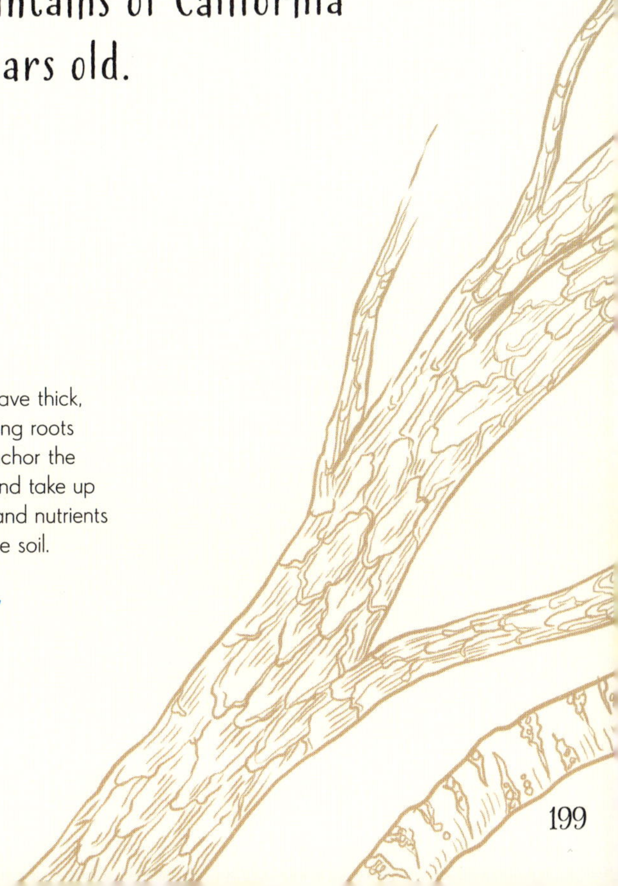

Trees have thick, spreading roots that anchor the trunk and take up water and nutrients from the soil.

Tree bark varies in colour and texture. The six types of bark shown here are from deciduous trees. From left to right, top to bottom: Tibetan cherry, redwood, silver birch, maple, plane, and beech.

Tundra plains cover about 20 per cent of the Earth's surface.

Tundra

The Arctic willow is one of the few flowering plants that can survive in the tundra.

The name "tundra" comes from the Finnish word *tunturia*, which means barren or treeless hill. Indeed, the tundra landscape lies bleak and frozen for most of the year. Even if a thin layer of soil does thaw, it isn't fertile enough for trees to grow.

Arctic tundra is found in areas near the North Pole, including Alaska, Iceland, and Siberia. This barren, treeless landscape is striking for a particular reason. In the summer months, patterns of many-sided shapes, called polygons, appear. They are made by the repeated freezing and thawing of the thin layer of moist soil on top of frozen or rocky ground. The layer of permanent frost, called permafrost, stops water draining away. Cracks in the ground freeze then thaw, and the water collects in the polygon-shaped pools.

In summer, polygonal patterns cover the flat surfaces of the tundra landscape of the Taymyr Peninsula in Siberia, Russia.

Tropical wetland

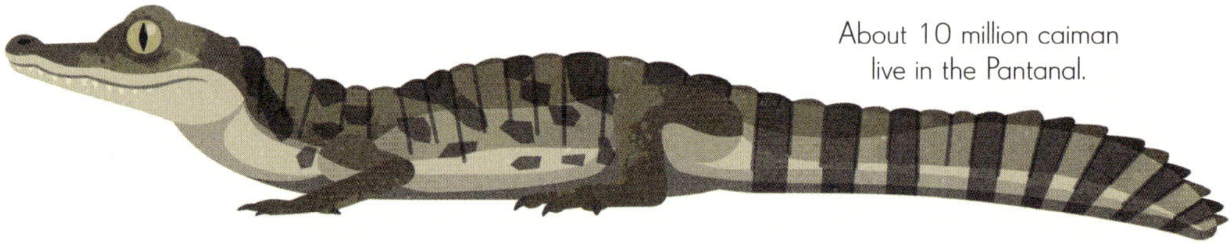

About 10 million caiman live in the Pantanal.

"Pantanal" comes from the Portuguese word *pântano*, meaning "big swamp".

During the wet season, the tropical wetland of the Pantanal covers parts of Brazil, Bolivia, and Paraguay.

For part of the year at least, the Pantanal in South America is the largest freshwater tropical wetland in the world. In the wet season – between November and March – warm, tropical rains blow across from the surrounding mountains and flood the area, causing the water level to rise. The grasslands get soaked, and marshes and lagoons develop.

The flooding makes the Pantanal very fertile, and an amazing variety of nearly 5,000 plant and animal species live here. After March, when the Pantanal starts to dry out, there is more land, but less water. The ponds get smaller and the fish have to swim closer together. Birds flock to catch them. Later, in the dry season, grasses grow again on the rich, fertile soil that was once under the floodwater.

Mangrove swamp

Mangrove trees are halophytic, which means "salt-loving".

There are about 80 different species of mangrove trees.

On warm tropical coasts around the world, mangrove trees grow in the sand and mud. Mangroves are an unusual type of tree because they can thrive in salt water. They have long and tangled roots that help anchor them to the mud, and that also breathe air when the water level is so low that the roots are no longer underwater. The leaves are unusual, too – they are thick and waxy, which helps stop the salt from drying them out.

Over time, mangrove roots branch out and build whole stretches of forests, protecting areas from coastal storms. Many animals make their home here – clambering among the roots and branches, swimming in the water, or burying themselves in the mud and sand.

This mangrove swamp is in Los Haitises National Park in the Dominican Republic.

Rice terraces

A rice plant takes five months to grow from seed to ripened plant and is then ready to be harvested.

Green and beautiful rice terraces are carved into the hillsides on the island of Luzon in the Philippines. They were made by the Ifugao people who have lived there for thousands of years. Nestling among the rice terraces are Ifugao villages, with farmers' houses called *bales*, and grain stores known as *alang*.

The slopes are too steep for the farmers to grow crops, so step-like terraces have been built, with walls made of stone or mud. The flat areas, called rice terrace paddies, are used for growing rice. When it rains, water from the forests at the tops of the mountains is guided downhill along channels to ponds that feed the rice terraces. All the villagers look after the ponds, terraces, and water channels year after year, so the people always have enough rice. Each generation teaches the next, so the children will know what to do in the future.

The rice terraces of Luzon are more than 2,000 years old.

These Ifugao rice terraces are in the village of Batad, in the north of the island of Luzon.

In the polder system, ditches were dug to drain the water and reclaim the land. While windmills were once used to pump the water, electric pumps are more common today.

Creating land

The "Netherlands" means "lower countries" and true to its name, a large part of this European country is near or below sea level. Because of this, the Netherlands has always faced the risk of flooding. So, about 2,500 years ago, the people living in the region piled up mounds of earth and built their houses on them to keep them dry. They called these mounds "terpen". To keep the terpen safe, they built small walls, called dykes, around them. Later, they drained the land and used windmills to pump water away along canals. This new, dry, reclaimed land they called polders. This practice continues today, only now, electric pumps, along with dykes, dams, and storm-surge barriers, all work together to protect the polders.

About 20 per cent of the Netherlands has been reclaimed from the sea.

The polder landscape of Polder Wormer Jisp en Nek is 19 km (12 miles) north of Amsterdam in the Netherlands.

Glossary

algae type of aquatic plant-like organism with no stems or leaves

algal bloom large mass of microalgae in a body of water

alloy metal that is made by mixing two or more types of metals together

asperitas cloud low-level clouds that ripple, like ocean waves

atmosphere layers of gases surrounding the Earth

calcite colourless or white mineral found in sedimentary and metamorphic rocks

caldera large crater formed after a volcano erupts and later collapses

continental crust layer of rock that makes up continental land and the surrounding shallow continental shelf

continental shelf part of a continent lying under ocean

core made mostly of nickel and iron, the solid inner core of the Earth is surrounded by a liquid outer core

crater lake body of water sitting inside a circular volcanic crater

crust outer layer of the Earth above the mantle, including both continental crust and oceanic crust

cumulonimbus cloud also known as a thundercloud, the only type that can make rain, hail, thunder, and lightning

current direction that the water is moving, in an ocean or river

deciduous tree or shrub that sheds its leaves seasonally

earthquake released pressure that occurs when two tectonic plates get stuck moving past each other

ecosystem all plants and animals that live together within a specific type of environment

epicentre point on the Earth's surface directly above the focus of an earthquake

erosion gradual breakdown and removal of rock or soil by water, wind, and/or ice

fault fracture where rocks have moved past one another

fault block mountain resulting from one block of land being pushed over another, as the land moves together

fissure crack in the ground

floodplain flat area of land by a river that floods

focus point underground where an earthquake starts

fog drip water droplets from clouds, which land on tree leaves and make them wet

fogbow light phenomenon that occurs when sunlight is spread by tiny water droplets in fog, appearing white or faint in colour

fold mountain rock layers that are pushed together and bend upwards to make a mountain

frazil ice substance consisting of tiny needle-shaped crystals, formed by supercooled water

geologist scientist who studies the origins, structure, and materials that make up Earth

geothermal activity hot magma heating up water from underground

glacier layers of snowfall piled up on a frozen river of ice that flows downhill under its own weight

glaze event alternative term for an ice storm

hydrothermal vent fissure in deep ocean floor often near volcanic activity where hot, mineral-laden fluids escape

icebox produced when sunlight is reflected by ice crystals into the sky, making a white or colourful halo of light

igneous rock formed from solidified magma or lava

lava molten magma that has erupted onto the Earth's surface from volcanoes or fissures in the ground

lenticular cloud disc-shaped clouds that stack up in the sky, often seen near mountainous areas

maelstrom large, powerful whirlpool

magma hot molten rock formed in the Earth's mantle and crust

mammatus cloud middle-level cloud that is bulbous in shape and often a sign of thundery weather

mantle layer of Earth between the crust and outer core

metamorphic rock formed from rocks changed by intense heat and/or pressure

meteor shooting star made from rock and space debris that burns up while travelling through Earth's atmosphere

meteorite meteor that has landed on Earth

microalgae tiny plant-like organisms that live in both ocean and freshwater

mid-oceanic ridge underwater mountain chain where new oceanic crust is made

Moho boundary boundary between the Earth's crust and mantle

Mohs hardness scale scale by which we measure the relative hardness (scratchability) of minerals, introduced by Friedrich Mohs

moonbow light phenomenon made from moonlight shining on water droplets, only occurring at night

nacreous cloud clouds that are pink in colour and only seen at the polar regions

natron salt from volcanic rock that makes water alkaline

noctilucent cloud high-level clouds that appear after sunset on warm summer evenings

oasis source of water in a hot, dry desert

oceanic crust layer of Earth's crust found under the ocean

ooze deep ocean seafloor sediments

ore rock from which a metal can be extracted

oxbow lake U-shaped lake or pool, left when a loop of river is cut off from the main river

permafrost layer of ground that stays frozen for years

piedmont glacier fan-shaped glacier that spreads out at the base of a hill

pneumatocysts floating air-filled sacs on the fronds of seaweed, like kelp

pyroclast rock formed by explosive volcanic eruptions, such as lava blocks, lapilli, and volcanic dust

rapids fast-flowing water rushing over a shallow and rocky riverbed

river delta triangle-shaped floodplain on flat land near the sea

sedimentary rock formed from compressed, hardened and cemented sediments, such as limestone and sandstone

sink hole holes in the surface of soft rock, created by rainwater wearing it away

speleothem natural rock formation formed in a cave, such as stalagmite, stalactite, or cave pearl

stratocumulus cloud common cloud, white and puffy in appearance

stratovolcano steep-sided volcano made of layers of erupted lava and ash

striated iceberg striped iceberg, such as one with blue and white stripes

supercooling lowering of the temperature of a liquid below freezing point, without it turning solid

troposphere lowest layer of the Earth's atmosphere

tsunami huge waves caused by underwater earthquakes or landslides

weathering rocks at the Earth's surface broken down by ice, wind, water, heat, and chemicals, before being moved by erosion

Visual guide

Core, page 8

Mantle, page 10

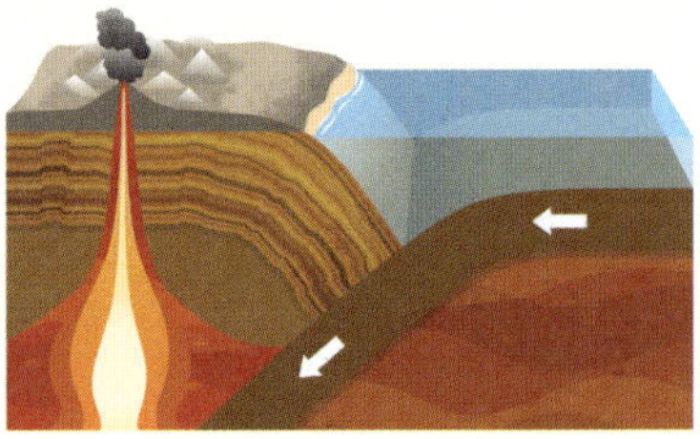

Rocky crust, page 12

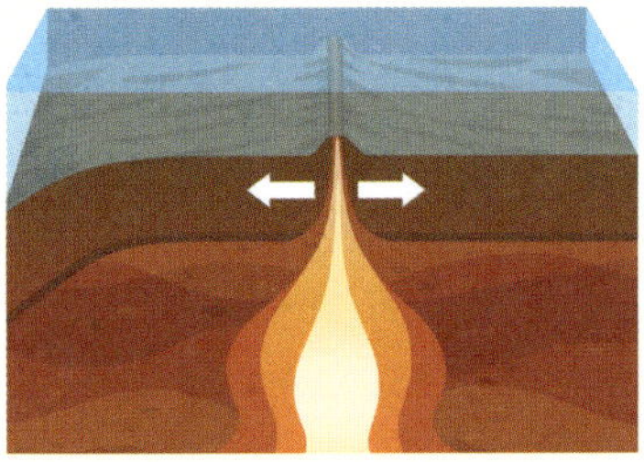

Giant's path, page 14

Meteor Crater, page 16

Devils Tower, page 20

Rainbow rocks, page 22

Fossils, page 24

Marble, page 26

Metals, page 28

Amethyst, page 32

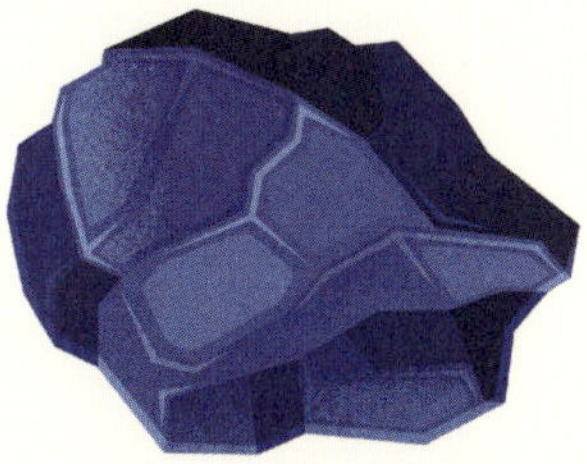
Diamond, page 34

Between two plates, page 40

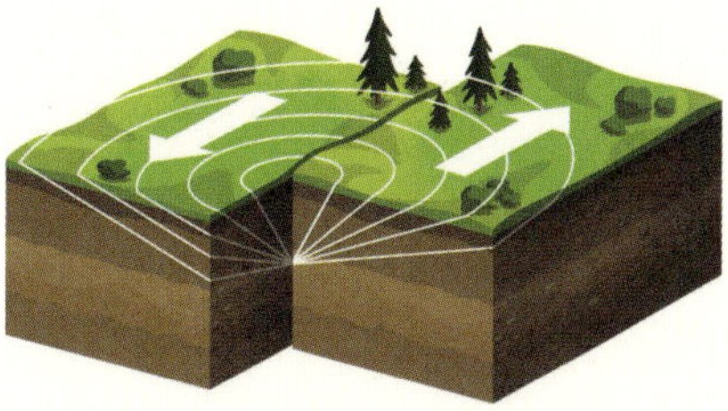
Fault line, page 42

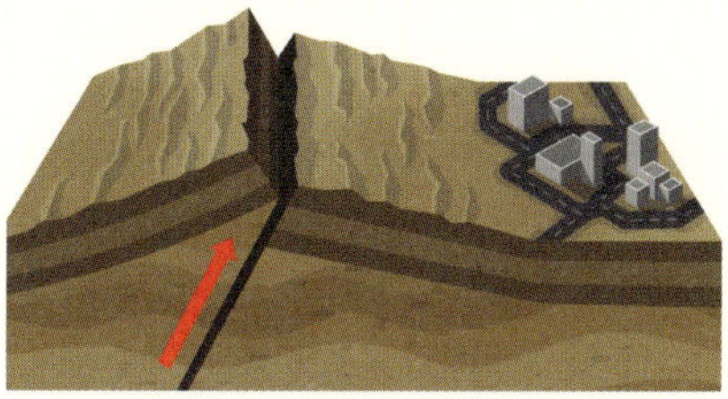
Rising mountains, page 44

Folding rock, page 46

Salt dome, page 48

Child of Krakatau, page 50

Ash cloud, page 52

Pahoehoe lava, page 54

A'a lava, page 56

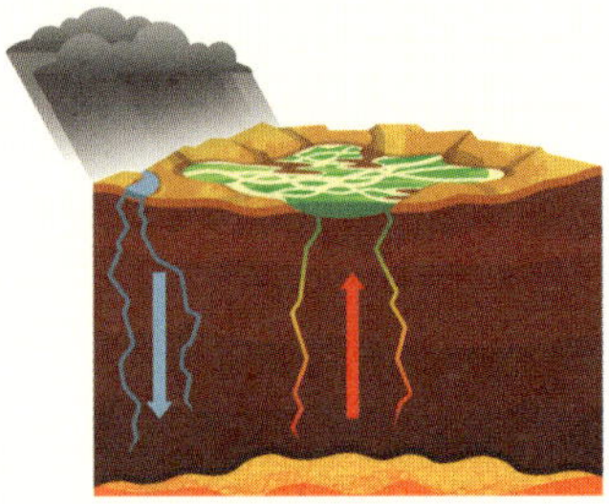

Acid pools, page 58

Geyser, page 60

Volcanic island, page 64

Sea stacks, page 66

Shaping stone, page 68

Honeycomb weathering, page 70

Chalk cliffs, page 72

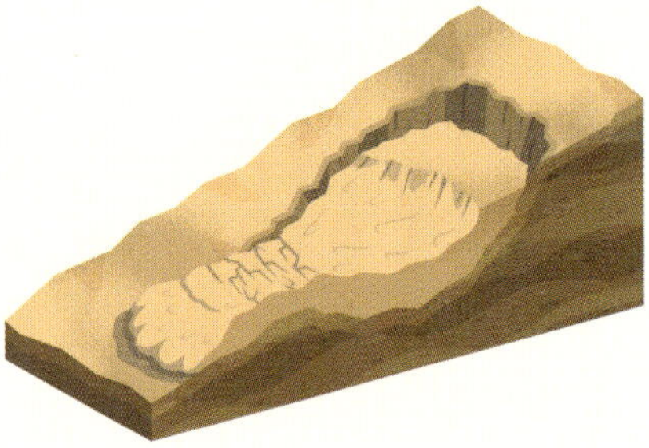

Landslide, page 74

Avalanche, page 76

Braided river, page 82

River shapes, page 84

River delta, page 86

Liquid Rainbow, page 88

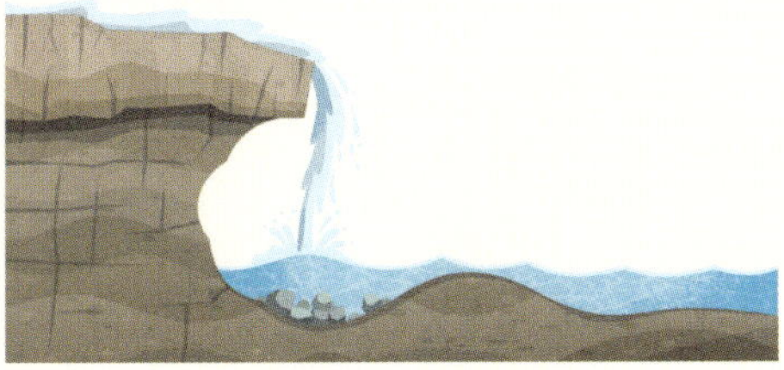
Waterfall, page 90

Salt lake, page 92

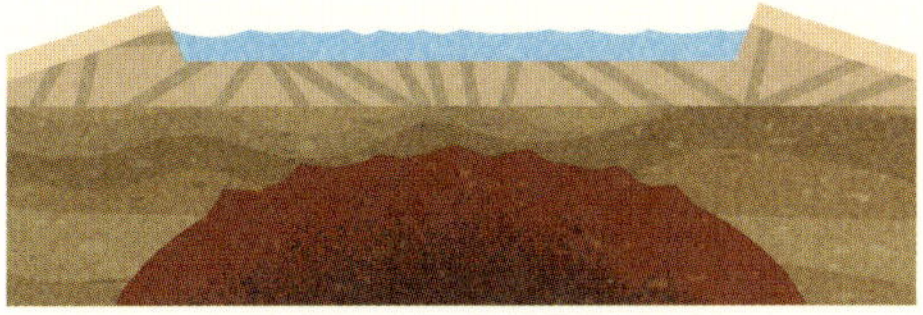
Crater Lake, page 94

Fjord, page 96

Giant cave, page 98

Speleothems, page 100

Cave pearls, page 102

Smoking chimneys, page 106

Manganese nodules, page 108

Ocean ooze, page 110

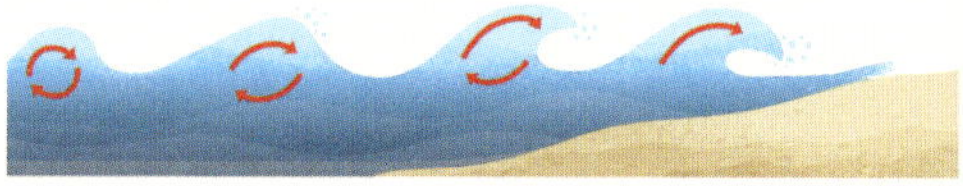

Waves, page 112

Whirlpool, page 114

Coral reef, page 116

Coral atoll, page 118

Kelp forest, page 120

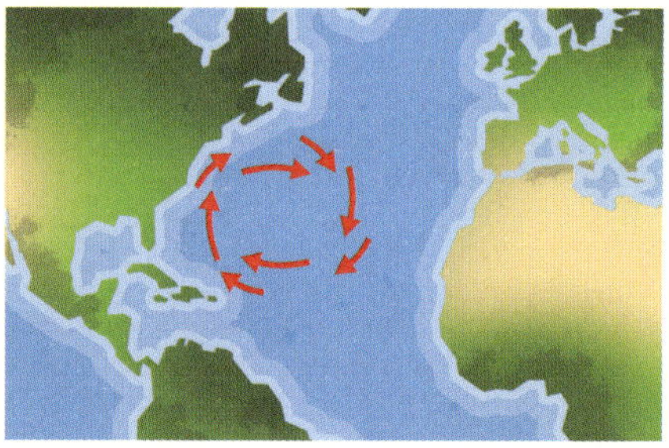

Sargassum, page 122

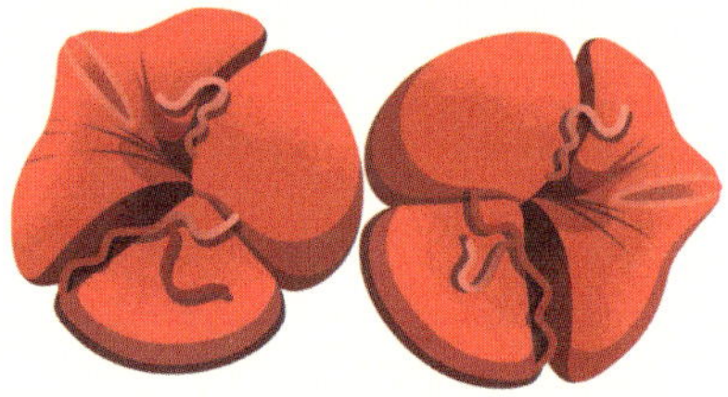

Red tide, page 124

Snow monsters, page 128

Glacier, page 130

Sea ice, page 132

Stripy iceberg, page 134

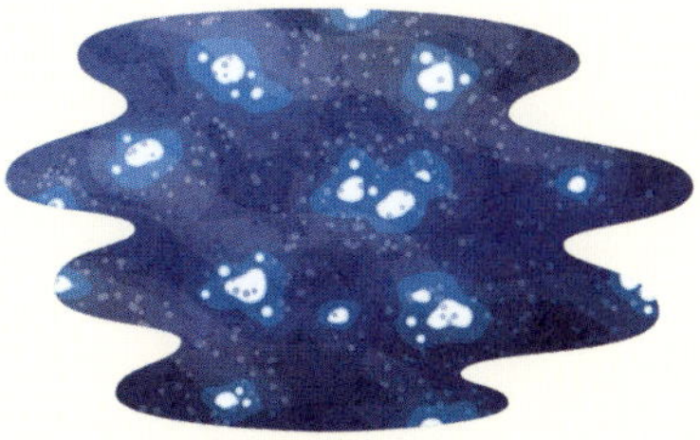

Blue ice, page 136

Ice cave, page 138

Frozen waterfall, page 140

Auroras, page 146

Wind, page 148

Clouds, page 150

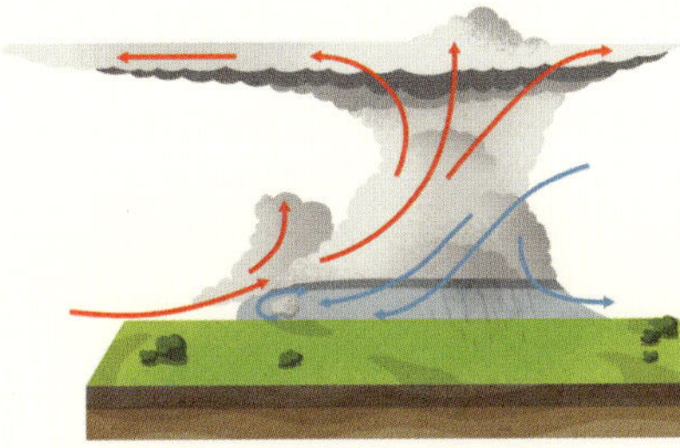

Storm cloud, page 152

Rain, page 154

Tornado, page 156

Fog, page 158

Hailstone, page 160

Ice storm, page 162

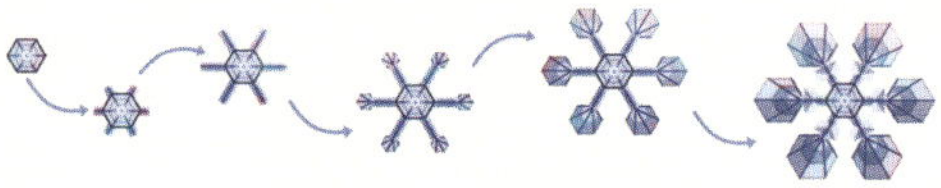
Snowflakes, page 164

Rainbow, page 166

Bows and halos, page 168

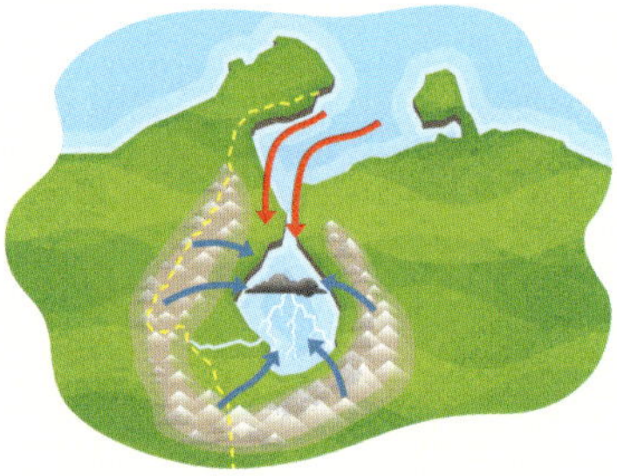
Everlasting storm, page 170

Mudcracks, page 172

Hot desert, page 178

Cold desert, page 180

Mushroom rock, page 182

Sand, page 184

Karst, page 186

Savanna, page 188

Temperate forest, page 190

Rainbow eucalyptus, page 192

Cloud forest, page 194

Taiga, page 196

Forest trees, page 198

Tundra, page 200

Tropical wetland, page 202

Mangrove swamp, page 204

Rice terraces, page 206

Creating land, page 208

Index

DK | Penguin Random House

Senior editor Marie Greenwood
Designers Brandie Tully-Scott, Kanika Kalra
Additional editorial Manisha Majithia
Senior jacket designer Elle Ward
Senior picture researcher Sakshi Saluja
DTP designers Vijay Kandwal, Dheeraj Singh
Managing editor Jonathan Melmoth
Managing art editors Diane Peyton Jones, Ivy Sengupta
Senior production editor Nikoleta Parasaki
Production controller John Casey
Jacket coordinator Magda Pszuk
Publishing director Sarah Larter

Consultant Dr Rebecca Williams

First published in Great Britain in 2023 by
Dorling Kindersley Limited
DK, One Embassy Gardens, 8 Viaduct Gardens,
London, SW11 7BW

The authorised representative in the EEA is
Dorling Kindersley Verlag GmbH. Arnulfstr. 124,
80636 Munich, Germany

10 9 8 7 6 5 4 3 2 1
001–333000–Oct/2023

A CIP catalogue record for this book
is available from the British Library.
ISBN: 978-0-2415-8537-5

Printed and bound in China

For the curious
www.dk.com

DK would like to thank: Kieran Jones and Abi Maxwell for editorial assistance; Charlotte Jennings and Bettina Myklebust Stovne for additonal design; Caroline Hunt for proofreading; Helen Peters for the index; Lynne Murray for picture library assistance; Daniel Long for the feature illustrations; Angela Rizza for the pattern and cover illustrations; Tuba Syed for metatagging.

About the author:

Cally Oldershaw is a geologist and gemmologist. She is the author of 15 books on gemstones, and has also published books on Earth science topics, including volcanoes, earthquakes, and oceans and seas. Cally has appeared on TV and radio and was the Curator of Gemstones at the Natural History Museum in London.

Picture credits

The publisher would like to thank the following for their kind permission to reproduce their photographs:
(Key: a-above; b-below/bottom; c-centre; f-far; l-left; r-right; t-top)

4 Alamy Stock Photo: Alexisaj (tl); Elizabeth Nunn (tr). **Dreamstime.com:** Baloncici (bl); Bjrn Wylezich (br). **6-7 Science Photo Library:** Gary Hincks (c). **8-9 Dreamstime.com:** PhotoChur. **10 Alamy Stock Photo:** E.R. Degginger. **12-13 Dreamstime.com:** Maciej Bledowski (b). **14-15 Getty Images / iStock:** benedek. **16-17 Science Photo Library:** Herve Conge, ISM. **18 Dorling Kindersley:** Oxford University Museum of Natural History (cl). **20-21 Shutterstock.com:** Edwin Verin. **22-23 Getty Images:** kittisun kittayacharoenpong. **24-25 Dorling Kindersley:** Royal Tyrrell Museum of Palaeontology, Alberta, Canada (b). **26-27 Getty Images:** Sian Seabrook. **28 Dreamstime.com:** Bjrn Wylezich (b). **28-29 Dreamstime.com:** Bjrn Wylezich (tc). **29 Dreamstime.com:** Bjrn Wylezich. **30 Dorling Kindersley:** Oxford University Museum of Natural History (bl). **31 Dorling Kindersley:** Natural History Museum, London (bc). **Dreamstime.com:** Geografika (bl). **32 Dreamstime.com:** Bohuslav Jelen. **34 Dreamstime.com:** Roberto Junior (r). **35 Dreamstime.com:** Thelightwriter (l). **36 Alamy Stock Photo:** Kip Evans (tl). **AWL Images:** Guy Edwardes (tr). **Getty Images:** Monica Bertolazzi (b); Jim Sugar (tc). **41 Alamy Stock Photo:** Martin Strmiska. **42 Alamy Stock Photo:** Phil Degginger. **44-45 4Corners:** Bernd Grundmann. **46-47 Alamy Stock Photo:** Matthijs Wetterauw. **48-49 Alamy Stock Photo:** Saeed Abdolizadeh. **50-51 Shutterstock.com:** Deni_Sugandi. **53 AWL Images:** Frank Krahmer. **54-55 Getty Images:** Matt Anderson Photography. **57 Alan Cressler. 59 Alamy Stock Photo:** Zoonar / Artush Foto. **60-61 Getty Images:** Nikolay Pandev / EyeEm. **62 Alamy Stock Photo:** Vincent M / Andia (bl); LWM / NASA / LANDSAT (tl). **Robert Harding Picture Library:** Planet Observer (crb). **63 Alamy Stock Photo:** Planet Observer / Universal Images Group North America LLC (c). **Getty Images / iStock:** graphixel (br). **64 AWL Images:** Marco Bottigelli. **66-67 Dreamstime.com:** Taras Vyshnya. **68-69 Dreamstime.com:** Minnystock. **70-71 Shutterstock.com:** Fotimageon. **72-73 Getty Images / iStock:** Alphotographic. **74-75 Alamy Stock Photo:** Adelheid Nothegger / imageBROKER. **76 Shutterstock.com:** Andrei Kovin. **78 Alamy Stock Photo:** Martin Strmiska (t). AWL Images: Frank Krahmer (cr). **Dreamstime.com:** Anna Komissarenko (br); Pniesen (bl). **82-83** Andre Ermolaev. **84-85** Alaska Region U.S. Fish & Wildlife Service: Kristine Sowl. **86-87 Getty Images:** Planet Observer / Universal Images. **88-89 Alamy Stock Photo:** travel4pictures. **90-91 Dreamstime.com:** Catherina Unger. **92-93 Alamy Stock Photo:** Alexander Bee. **94-95 Getty Images / iStock:** JeffGoulden (b). **96 Getty Images / iStock:** tomch. **98 Getty Images:** Ryan H / 500px. **101 Robert Harding Picture Library:** Nick Upton. **102-103 Robert Harding Picture Library:** Ryan Deboodt. **104 123RF.com:** Chonlasub Woravichan (tc/Sea Turtle). **Alamy Stock Photo:** Brandon Cole Marine Photography (crb); MYN / Sheri Mandel / Nature Picture Library (cl). **Dreamstime.com:** Ingvars (tl); Krzysztof Odziomek (tc, tr); Harvey Stowe (ca). **naturepl.com:** David Shale (cr). **105 123RF.com:** willyambradberry (tc). **Alamy Stock Photo:** David Shale / Nature Picture Library (cr); Adisha Pramod (cb). **naturepl.com:** David Shale (br). **107 MARUM- Center for Marine Environmental Sciences, University of Bremen:** Center for Marine Environmental Sciences, University of Bremen (CC-BY 4.0). **108-109 Science Photo Library:** NOAA Office Of Ocean Exploration And Research, 2019 Southeastern Us Deep-Sea Exploration. **110 Science Photo Library:** Steve Gschmeissner. **112-113 Getty Images** / iStock: Philip Thurston. **115 Getty Images:** Ray Massey. **116-117 Getty Images / iStock:** cinoby. **118-119 Getty Images** / iStock: Zhao Liu. **120-121 Getty Images:** Douglas Klug. **122-123 Dreamstime.com:** Massimilianofinzi. **125 Science Photo Library:** Bill Bachman. **126 Alamy Stock Photo:** H. Mark Weidman Photography (bl). **Dreamstime.com:** Martyn Unsworth (c). **Science Photo Library:** Louise Murray (cl). **127 123RF.com:** Raldi Somers / gentoomultimedia (bc). **Alamy Stock Photo:** Andr Gilden (tr); RIEGER Bertrand / hemis.fr (cl). **Dreamstime.com:** Andrei Stepanov (cr). **128-129 Getty Images:** David Mareuil / Anadolu Agency. **130-131 Shutterstock.com:** Nicolaj Larsen (b). **132-133 Florian Ledoux Photography. 134 Alamy Stock Photo:** Martin Harvey. **136-137 Alamy Stock Photo:** Eric Dietrich / Hedgehog House / Minden Pictures. **138 Getty Images:** coolbiere photograph. **141 AWL Images:** Tom Mackie. **142 Dreamstime.com:** Tawatchai Prakobkit (t). **Getty Images:** Martin Harvey (cr). **Getty Images / iStock:** heathernemec (br). **Science Photo Library:** Jim Reed Photography (cl). **144 Dreamstime.com:** Wisconsinart (cra). **145 123RF.com:** Leonello Calvetti (cr). **Alamy Stock Photo:** D. Hurst (cra). Photolibrary: Corbis (ca). **146 Alamy Stock Photo:** Robert Haasmann / imageBROKER. **148-149 Alamy Stock Photo:** mauritius images GmbH. **150 Alamy Stock Photo:** Per-Andre Hoffmann / Image Professionals GmbH (tr); Katho Menden (tl); Mike Grandmaison / All Canada Photos (bl). **Dreamstime.com:** Menno Van Der Haven (cl). **Getty Images:** Ozkan Bilgin / Anadolu Agency (cr). **152-153 Jim Reed Photography. 154-155 Alamy Stock Photo:** Nigel Roake. **156-157 Alamy Stock Photo:** Jason Persoff Stormdoctor / Cultura Creative Ltd. **158-159 Alamy Stock Photo:** David Wall. **160 Alamy Stock Photo:** Silvia Bragagnolo / EyeEm. **162-163 Getty Images / iStock:** carlosbezz. **164 Science Photo Library**: Kenneth Libbrecht (cl, bl, cr). **165 Science Photo Library:** Kenneth Libbrecht (tl, tr). **166 Alamy Stock Photo:** Andy Rouse / Nature Picture Library. **168 Dreamstime.com:** Chayanan Phumsukwisit (b). **Getty Images:** Martin Ruegner (c). naturepl.com: Erlend Haarberg (t). **171 Alamy Stock Photo:** Tourism Ministry / Xinhua. **172-173 Getty Images / iStock:** temizyurek. **174 Getty Images:** Timothy Allen (bc); Arturo Castaneyra (t); Tim Hester / EyeEm (ca). naturepl.com: Ugo Mellone (cb). **176 Alamy Stock Photo:** Don Johnston_ON (cb). **Dreamstime.com:** Erectus (cra); Sergey Korotkov (ca); Positivetravelart (crb). **177 Dreamstime.com:** Antonpetrus (cra); George Burba (cla); Max5128 (ca); Hel080808 (crb); Zorro12 (clb); Eugen Haag (cb). **178-179 Alamy Stock Photo:** Ernie Janes / Nature Picture Library (b). **180-181 Alamy Stock Photo:** TravelCollection / Image Professionals GmbH. **182-183 Getty Images / iStock:** cinoby. **184 Science Photo Library:** Dirk Wiersma (tl). **184-185 Dreamstime.com:** Sergey Kolesnikov (c). **185 Dreamstime.com:** µ € (tr). **Science Photo Library:** Dirk Wiersma (cr). **186-187 Getty Images / iStock:** aphotostory. **188-189 Alamy Stock Photo:** Eric Baccega / naturepl.com (b). **190-191 Getty Images / iStock:** DenisTangneyJr. **192 Shutterstock.com:** gg-foto. **194-195 naturepl.com:** Nick Hawkins. **196-197 Getty Images / iStock:** Onfokus. **198 Alamy Stock Photo:** Krystyna Szulecka Photography (cr). **Getty Images:** Wolfgang Filser / EyeEm (br); Louise Docker Sydney Australia (tl); Gado Images (tr); Arterra / Universal Images Group (cl); Jordan Lye (bl). 200-201 **Dreamstime.com:** Vladimir Melnik. **202-203 Getty Images:** Natphotos. **204-205 Alamy Stock Photo:** Kevin Schafer / Minden Pictures. **206-207 Dreamstime.com:** Rodrigolab. **208 Alamy Stock Photo:** frans lemmens

Cover images: *Front:* **Alamy Stock Photo:** Thomas Marent / Minden Pictures cla; **Dorling Kindersley:** Natural History Museum, London crb; **Dreamstime.com:** Olga Khoroshunova cra, Monkeygreen cr, Rumos tc; **Getty Images / iStock:** cinoby bl; **Science Photo Library:** Steve Gschmeissner ca